Green Water Strategy

The New Paradigm in Modern Business

Green Water Strategy

The New Paradigm in Modern Business

T. Barrington Frank, BA, VMP
D. Wayne Willard, BS, PMP, VMP

Green Water Strategy

ISBN-13: 978-1477698495

Dedication

To our families, friends, co-workers past and present who put up with our quirky ways;

To our teachers who introduced us to the tools of learning;

To our managers, bosses and leaders who gave us opportunities to grow professionally,

Thanks to each and every one whose ears we bent and whose patience we challenged in pursuit of our goal.

TABLE OF CONTENTS

OUR PURPOSE

Are you a consumer wondering how the multitude of questionable products makes it to your attention? Are you an investor wondering what is up (or down) with your favorite company's stock price? Are you an employee feeling like a ball in a giant pachinko machine, bouncing and careening randomly? Do you feel stuck in a dead-end job? Are you not even sure you will be able to *keep* your dead-end job? Are you a manager trapped in a cul-de-sac on the organization chart, doomed eventually to run the cafeteria? Are you tired of feeling left out? Weary of feeling as if you just don't fit in and can't understand what is happening around you? Would you like to take a step that jump-starts your career? Perhaps just save your career?

If any of these statements are familiar, then *Green Water Strategy* will explain to you the new age business practices that foster these feelings. It will also explain why those practices exist and why they persist. Study the Green Water principles and learn how you can adopt those principles to put (or keep) money in your pocket. And if that's not enough for you, understand this evolving world and perhaps you can add a new title on your business card and even see your name on the door to that corner office.

Take the step that propels you into the future! Take the step that maximizes your paycheck and your opportunities! Turn the pages of this volume and learn the secrets of Green Water Success and Survival. Let this book provide you with "just enough" information and skill to allow you to perform your job to ensure your next promotion.

Read, study and apply "just enough" competence to assume the identity of the modern day super-hero of the Green Water Corporation – the Veneer Manager. Whether you are managing a team, managing your career or just managing to make it into the office, this information is vital to your survival.

INTRODUCTION

First There Was the CSC

One dreary Monday morning I arrived at work and found a Dilbert cartoon clipped from that morning's paper and taped to my office door. As I stood and read it, I saw the handwritten abbreviation "CSC" and a roughly drawn rain cloud added to the third frame of the cartoon. I quickly read the captions, and chuckling at the humor, I knew immediately who had left the comic on my door. It was my friend and colleague Tom Frank. I also knew both what the CSC inscription meant and why he had made the connection with the cartoon. It was as though Scott Adams had been in yesterday's meeting.

At the time, Tom and I had known each other for nearly a quarter of a century, working together at two different companies for fifteen of those years. We shared a sense of frustration with many aspects of corporate life. We also shared a sense of humor and over the years developed a number of oddball but strangely believable theories for the logic-defying corporate shenanigans we continually encountered.

One such theoretical explanation we referred to as the CSC – The Cosmic Stupidity Cloud. This theory explained how management made decisions using faulty assumptions, without the bother of recognizing obvious facts or worrying about reaching rational conclusions based on those facts. Sometimes it seemed as if the Cosmic Stupidity Cloud caused those under its influence to ignore *all* facts as extraneous. We had observed that individuals as well as groups exhibited the effects of the CSC, the presence of which was either a signal of impending failure or a guarantee of that failure. Either way, doom was just around the corner. This malevolent cloud seemed to muddle the minds of managers and team members alike, encouraging them to make choices that were utterly incomprehensible. The cartoon that morning depicted a classic case of the Cosmic Stupidity Cloud influencing Dilbert's world as the "pointy-haired boss" once again sent the company ship into the path of a hurricane.

1

Standing there in front of my office door studying that cartoon was the moment the idea of Green Water Strategy was born. Also at that moment, our *personal* CSC lifted and we saw that over the years we had developed many management theories, unwritten rules and hidden concepts to account for the decisions and actions taken that invariably sent an organization in the wrong direction. Tom and I had created the CSC to explain the mysterious behavior of otherwise intelligent people. We immediately knew it was imperative that we communicate our discoveries to others.

The Genesis of an Idea

After spending nearly forty years apiece in the process-bound, massively redundant and multi-layered hierarchy that is Corporate America, it is time to document what we have learned and to codify it as our contribution to the science of management. This same need to explain the world around us has also spawned the likes of "Dilbert", the movie "Office Space" and the hit television show "30 Rock". We knew we were not the only ones compelled to speak up and were certainly not the first to call attention to the situation. However, we are the first to put a name to it, to offer an explanation as to why it exists and to suggest ways for the individual to cultivate it profitably.

In organizing our ideas into book form, we came to realize that the oddball theories we had developed served as at least a partial explanation for how many of the current business conditions came to be. As we built an outline of our work and considered how to present these ideas, we realized that what was originally an exercise in protecting our own sanity and having some fun, had turned into an eerily believable explanation for the stagnant economies and bankrupt governments prevalent at the beginning of the twenty-first century. The surprising result has been realizing that we had produced a broad overview of current management practices. Even more unexpected is the recognition that handled in the right manner, many of the precepts can paradoxically produce positive results when implemented in a controlled fashion.

Why You Need This Book

Our analysis has led to the conceptualization of a new business methodology that we have given the name "Green Water Strategy".

The activities outlined in this book flourish under the generic policies of this strategy. You need to understand not only how to identify the practices that are evidence of a Green Water Strategy (GWS), you also need to understand the theories behind the part science, part magic, part voodoo ritual that has become a standard set of modern business practices.

Green Water Strategy is the cotton candy for sale at the Project Management Carnival. Understanding this new world is the only way you can ensure your corporate survival in an ever less secure world. Having arrived at your current company because you needed a job, this work will help you understand how to keep it.

For those who do not think GWS will apply to their lives, consider this - there is a bit of folk wisdom that is widely circulated among airplane pilots. Roughly, it states that there are only two kinds of pilots: those who have experienced a gear-up landing and those who are going to experience a gear-up landing. We can say the same of business and government organizations. There are really only two kinds: those that are operating under the mantle of a Green Water Strategy and those that are *going* to be operating under the mantle of GWS. You may not like it – but it is here to stay.

The roots of the Green Water Strategy can be discerned in a watershed case study by Shepherd Mead published six decades ago (*How to Succeed in Business without Really Trying*, 1952). The work was a best-seller but thereafter languished for almost 10 years. In 1961, Mead's visionary observations were revised and presented by Abe Burrows and Frank Loesser in the form of a morality play masking its semi-Socratic dialogue and included a pseudo-Greek chorus, all of which was presented by a touring company.

More than half a century later, a fresh examination of management practices is warranted, given the radical differences between the twenty-first century business world and that of the mid-twentieth. The Green Water Strategy acknowledges its historical origins, updating and expanding on those earlier ideas to encompass the prevalent thinking of the new millennium.

Where possible, we will share examples from our personal and professional lives. Included throughout are letters from disoriented and desperate folks just like you who are struggling to understand the shifting corporate sands under their feet. Their examples should serve to help guide you through the mysteries of the Green Water Strategy.

We have also included a select number of chapters from the soon to be released *Green Water Strategy Manual*. This manual provides additional details to support GWS theories and concepts.

SETTING SAIL WITH A GREEN WATER STRATEGY

Launching the Lifeboat

Dear Mr. Frank and Mr. Willard –

To say I am puzzled is an understatement. I have observed our leadership convene meeting after meeting in which the discussion focuses on the need to probe deeper into the problem under consideration. There is always an appointed committee tasked with completing a "deep dive" analysis of the issue and a date set for a report out. The problem is, the report out never seems to happen.

Instead, the direction always seems to be a reaction to crisis with the solutions invariably being the quickest fix possible. Since crisis is always the driver, a rapid response seems to be the accepted methodology and the answers never quite meet the real needs. Can we just once actually look for the best solution and implement it?

Can you explain to me how we get off this treadmill?

Vexed in Vancouver
==========
Dear Vexed –

You company clearly operates under the Green Water Strategy. By that, we mean they are committed to looking for the quick fix. The less time and effort expended the better. Or at least that is the opinion of your leadership. The problem with that, of course, is the cost to both your customers and your teams when the response really just consists of slapping on a new coat of paint instead of pulling down the wall to see what the real problem is.

It's not you. And it's not just your company. The Green Water Strategy has taken the business world by storm. This is simply a reactive response that seems to seek out the fastest way to the finish line, driven mostly by the overwhelming complexity of finding the actual solution. Study our landmark work on Green Water Strategy enjoy the scenery as you cruise the shallow waters of the Green Ocean.

Frank and Willard

Explorers on the Corporate Frontier

The Green Water Strategy is a new paradigm for business environments. It includes a broad-based set of practices and procedures spawned by the unintentional acts of managers who are possessed by an economic imperative for survival in a hostile ecology. Contrary to most examples of Social Darwinism, these adaptations permit the less gifted and less talented to succeed simply by pretending to know what they are doing.

We derive the phrase "green water" from the color of shallow water found at the edge of the ocean. "Shallow" is the central principle behind every idea presented here. The Green Water Strategy, unlike the currently popular Blue Ocean and Red Ocean strategies, applies to much more than just market definition. GWS is a philosophy that includes all aspects of business and government and one that has appeared spontaneously. We have chosen this description to underline the theme of thin coating, least effort, and a minimalistic approach, which has taken hold of Corporate America and the public sector at every level.

Deep-water sailors are familiar with the term "blue water". The reference is to the cobalt blue color of the deep, open ocean water upon which they sail. It is common practice in the U.S. Navy, and a part of the inter-service rivalry to refer to the members of the Coast Guard as shallow water sailors. Some in the Navy have labeled them "green water sailors" after the color of those near-shore shallows. We do not believe this is intended as a compliment.

In spite of this attempted jab on the part of our naval military, it should be noted that in the ocean world, the shallow water is a much more productive and lively environment. The marine life in shallow water is more prevalent and diverse. Likewise, those shallow water sailors of the Coast Guard are a busy group, involved in many different things as they cruise near the shore. As a means to measure the relative level of activity, clearly the water depth can offer some insight. Green water foams and churns – it is very alive.

Green Water Strategy calls for a focus on minimalist business practices. This is contrary to the more widely accepted view of the "deep dive" as the accepted approach. Opportunities abound in the shallows where the scuba gear of a mega-corporation is not required to plumb the depths. A snorkel is sufficient and should you get in trouble you can always stand up.

Green Water Strategy also relates to the operational business model. A shallow approach to all things is the standard methodology to be observed in a business exhibiting Shallow Thought Practices. In this realm, development of an overall strategic direction that acknowledges Shallow Thought is called for. In addition, the individual at work in a Shallow Thought Business needs to consider the creation of his or her own Green Water Strategy that reflects their personal Green Water Survival or Green Water Success approach.

Deep Dive Paves the Way for Shallow Thought

In the dim recesses of history, when the first cave dweller recognized that his tribe had successfully completed a hunt for the Woolly Mammoth at his direction, he realized that even as a pant-less primate, he had knowledge to impart. Thus, the first MBA program was born. One can find credentials for the Mastodon Beast Abatement program painted on cave walls throughout Europe.

Following the introduction of Mammoth Hunting Schools around the world, the hunting business inexorably moved toward more and more complexity. First, it was new tools such as bigger and heavier spears. Then came the need to invent devices for launching those spears and before long, we had the anti-ballistic missile program. As ideas, skills, and technologies grew, making things more complex seemed a logical choice. The truth is, in most businesses today, there is a well-rooted belief that the answer to all the problems lies in the collection of more data, the discussion of more options, and the adoption of the latest complexities, process improvements and procedures. Complexity has come to be viewed as the answer to every problem. As we moved from mammoth hunters to missile launchers, the day to day business of making decisions has become harder and harder. In answer to the need to gain the kind of real-world knowledge believed to be necessary for decision making, the "deep dive" was created to collect ever greater amounts of data.

Deep diving is for explorers and treasure hunters. This methodology illustrates the "Vegas Principle of Random Success" in that it pays off just often enough to draw the player back again. Not everyone has a Glomar Explorer ready to plumb the depths of the world's economic oceans. Defining a strategy in support of the new view of "Thin" and "Shallow" is a necessity for the individual or company that hopes to survive in the current market. For an appreciation of how a Shallow Thought management style attempts to stack the deck in its approach to research & development, see "Patent Trolls: Why Bother to Create" in the *Green Water Strategy Manual*.

Businesses created the traditional and previously accepted model - the "deep dive" - by design. The belief that more information and more detail would generate more success resulted in the development of this approach. The Green Water Strategy, in contrast, is a naturally occurring and evolutionary concept that is not crafted by design. It has appeared and grown through natural events.

Today we see that many decisions made in business are based on an overarching principal expressed by the "deep dive". The phrase has even been collectivized into a single word with appropriately located capital letters that is trademarked by one of America's foremost management consulting companies. At times if feels as though when instituting a "deep dive", chants and incantations are invoked as part of the process, so firm is the belief that a miracle will follow.

Whether as a result of spiritual intervention or human agency, you can point to regulations and product changes that exist because of previous catastrophic events. In the auto industry, we have a history of accidents to thank for headlights, safety glass and seat belts. In the food industry, we have lawsuits to thank for the printed warning on our coffee cup as well as the safety stickers on meat products. It occurred to fiscally responsible executives everywhere that in-depth analysis and rigorously applied processes would reduce if not eliminate any product risk. The result has been a boon and a bane. Safer products do exist as a result. The "bane" came later.

Having found a useful methodology, organizations quickly began applying it to areas apart from risk analysis. This soon became the province of the MBA and process improvement specialists. Those groups advanced the procedures and with the collusion of the executives, developed reporting practices and evaluation measures for use across all projects within a business. The result of this was that individual managers had a 50/50 chance of having to follow procedures that did not relate to them or else participate in a constant revision of those procedures with each new project.

Over time, as old processes solidified, new processes accreted like calcium carbonate on a coral reef, or perhaps more aptly, attached themselves like barnacles to a ship's hull. Eventually the origins of the procedures were lost to history or at least obscured, and even though they were sometimes questioned, they were more often blindly followed. New product development tends to shrink in such an atmosphere. Blending a new and creative proposal with mandatory and regulatory ingredients in the corporate idea-cement-mixer will generate an unpalatable lump of dough as often as it might produce batter for an angel food cake.

Interestingly, "deep diving" is also the phrase used to refer to recreational scuba diving when one exceeds a depth of sixty feet. Regardless of which of the two interpretations of the phrase you care to assign – business or scuba - they both tend to result in the same outcomes when things go wrong. The "deep dive" has the unfortunate effect of magnifying any mistakes made. For example, simply imagine the result of running out of air while scuba diving at eighty feet as compared to ten feet. The deeper the dive the more dramatic the danger encountered. In shallow water, it does not take long to surface. From that perspective, shallow is safer and safer is better. In the business environment, having delved too deeply into a subject, the individual becomes swamped by details and frozen by the fear of making an insufficiently informed choice.

In the business world, "deep dive" is somewhat of a malapropism. Greater clarity is sought through a rigorous and in-depth examination – a literal submersion in an ocean of details. Anyone experienced with diving of any kind will immediately recognize the fallacy behind such nomenclature. Visibility, hence comprehension, is reduced by depth.

Depth only produces obscurity not the hoped for clarity. In the ocean world, in the first three feet, fifty per cent of the light has been absorbed. Only twenty per cent of the light reaches thirty feet and light is virtually non-existent at six hundred and sixty feet. In addition, the water filters out colors selectively as depth increases so the appearance of an object differs when compared to how it is viewed at the surface. Oceanographers have optimistically labeled the zone from the surface to six hundred and sixty feet as the "sunlight" zone and the next twenty-six hundred feet as the "twilight" zone. So the deeper we go, the more data we gather, the less we truly see. It is no wonder non-divers get confused on the "deep dive" topic.

The Shallow Thought Mindset

Recognizing that the time and energy we spend in our day-to-day activities in servicing our projects is excessive, the authors began to analyze all aspects of business decision making. Surprisingly, as our study progressed we found that many of the current ideas that demand greater detailed planning, more complicated statistical measurements, and additional levels of management can be readily challenged. And in fact, they are being challenged informally and without a recognized methodology as mid-level managers struggle to maintain their seats in today's stop-and-go, musical-chair, corporate world.

Businesses have known for a long time that there is a problem. Project failures are epidemic and development costs are high and unrecoverable without a product. Attempts have been made to solve this problem through the application of several different solutions.

The first has already been discussed – the "deep dive". This is a response to the "If only…" approach to analyzing the problem. If only more time was spent in requirements definition, in research, in market analysis – the list is endless. This approach to identifying the problem is rapidly overwhelmed by high volumes of data that will invariably suffer from multiple interpretations.

Another approach is a variation on the "deep dive" where the subject area is to be more limited in scope but still studied intensively. This is a form of process improvement studies, which are referred to as "lean workouts". The goal of such investigations is to identify process bottlenecks and recommend changes. Some organizations report success using this methodology but later analysis often shows that such reports reveal a bias on the part of the participants. Too often, the analysis is colored by a preconceived notion of the problem and the solution and those reporting success are usually those who authored the chosen solution.

A third approach is the application of rigorous and somewhat standardized project management principles. While stringent PM processes have resulted in some success, there exist unfortunate information overloads with this solution as well. This area is studied in detail in the chapter *Managing Projects*.

The search for answers with these methods is unproductive because the purpose is more often to fix blame rather than correct the reasons for failure. The result of all these approaches seems to be the generation of work for other people, which might be okay if the intention was to create an internal Jobs Program on the way back to full employment.

Discovering the Green Tide

Flourishing in the shallows of the Green Water Strategy is a new and vigorous form of management philosophy and style. When biologists discover a new species of plant or animal, they have the privilege of naming it. Usually the name is a combination of an existing genus and the new species name that reflects either the geographic location of the discovery, or a Latinized version of the discoverer's name – like *frankii* or *washingtonia*. We are the "biologists" that have uncovered a new "corporate life form" so we claim the privilege of giving it a name. We call this new concept Veneer Management – *lamina factotum* – and abbreviate it as VM. The Latin phrase literally translates as "veneer manager". At least we offer that translation according to our rights as discoverers. Further, according to the rules of VM-Linguistics, we can adopt this name because we say we can. This is an important concept within the world of Veneer Management – the ability to define rules to suit the moment.

VM describes the set of business practices operating under the Green Water Strategy. These practices are a natural outgrowth of the increasing complexity of business in the new millennium. Business in the world of Veneer Management is about knowing less and doing less, yet sustaining the confident appearance of progress and even success. The combination of the Green Water Strategy and the practice of Veneer Management will reduce a manager's purpose to either of two simple goals, defined as VM-Survival or VM-Success. Managers who desire to perfect the art of pretending to understand what they are doing reduce their workload and ride the wave to success or survival, by adopting VM. Peel back the "veneer" of many successful business people and you will discover they do not know their backside from a hot rock but they do know how to project the image of success.

A Word of Caution

We must issue a word of caution. The Green Water Strategy contains elements that are both subtle and beguiling. Many businesses exhibit different facets of the strategy but few if any were developed with GWS in mind. The entry point is rarely the business as a whole but through individual managers who turn to these practices out of necessity. Feeling compelled to function in situations for which they are unprepared they assume the veil of a VM-Manager with relative ease. Adopting this philosophy is nearly effortless and will appear rewarding to the practitioner. It allows the untutored and less knowledgeable to reach positions of influence regardless of real competency. The effects then multiply across management teams until the overall business strategy has been altered and the GWS has arrived.

From time to time, we have noted that as we were writing this book we would slip between a VM-Promotional-Mode and a VM-Criticism-Mode without any awareness of having done so. We have retained some aspects of this posture in various parts of the book both as an object lesson to the reader and because there are those VM-Activities that are at times oddly successful. While we consider ourselves observers and sometimes supporters of Green Water Strategy and Veneer Management, it is imperative to understand the inherent dangers of adopting VM without thoroughly understanding the nature of such practices. Our warning to you is simply one of care. It is tempting to implement VM-Practices across the board into your business without understanding the implications. Be on your guard.

Having provided a high-level overview of Green Water Strategy as a corporate way of life, we will now delve a bit deeper into the history of this revolutionary approach. But first, a quick review of what we have discussed to this point.

Summary

Each of the main segments of this book will end with a summarization of the ideas contained in that section. This will serve as a review of the major points to reinforce the concepts.

Green Water Strategy is our description of the new wave of operational practices sweeping the coastline of American business and government, freeing it from the burden of over-analysis and over-thinking while remaining open to the possibilities inherent in a rapidly shifting tide of economic and organizational change.

The Green Water Strategy represents the outcome of the historic struggle between two opposing approaches to business. The first, driven by the idea of in-depth analysis is the traditional solution where a business is inevitably bound up in a net of practice, process and procedure. The second, driven by a rapid dipping and rising into and above the ocean of details is considerably more agile and more responsive

Veneer Management has been identified as a new philosophy in the approach to managing under the Green Water Strategy. A simplified focus on either goal of survival or success in this environment pares a manager's effort to the essentials.

By carefully studying the text, charts and graphs, the VM-Manager will be able to apply the thin skin of logic presented here to whatever business model is being addressed. Being alert to any signs of an impending "deep dive" state makes possible a return to the safety of shallower water. By employing Veneer Management consistently, and by remembering not to fall victim to the temptation to over analyze, over plan, or over organize, the VM-Manager will chart a course to personal success or survival.

Adoption of Veneer Management principles and practices is a risky venture for the untutored. Because of the inherent nature of "less" knowledge, time and skill, an incorrectly implemented VM-Business Model can be disastrous. On the other hand, the appeal of this approach is clear when success is achieved.

VENEER MANAGEMENT – AN ENABLING MECHANISM

Launching the Lifeboat

Dear Mr. Frank and Mr. Willard –

My manager for the last 26 months has been replaced – just when it seemed he was beginning to understand the business - by a kid who could be my grandson. Other "wet-behind-the-ears" managers have been put in place who do not seem to know enough to come in out of the rain. Their resumes can't be anything but short, which for me, speaks to the level of management skill and the business expertise they bring. I hear the new guy recite the important management buzzwords but I don't think he has a clue what they mean in a real business environment.

Our division is but one of many in the parent corporation's diverse portfolio of companies. But for crying out loud – this latest guy managed a fleet of food trucks and we manufacture extruded aluminum products. I sense no aptitude in this fellow for running the business and get a strong impression that this is a temporary stop on his journey to a more important and higher paying position. Where is the benefit in this? Is "syn-ergy" spelled with an "I"?

Confused in Cleveland
==========
Dear Confused -

You need to get over the gunwale and down the gangplank and go sit on the beach. Your company is but one in the fleet of watercraft the corporation has cast afloat in the shoals of their Green Water Strategy. In doing so, they have fully embraced the shallow approach to operations and have implemented Veneer Management principles as part of their tactics for reaching success through the minimalization of effort.

You need to understand the opportunity this actually brings to you. As this manager will not understand anything that you do, you are able to execute any plan you believe appropriate as long as it dovetails into his goal of reporting success and moving ahead. You can still do the right things as you see them but don't expect to be rewarded. As we all know, in a VM Business environment, "It doesn't pay to do the right thing." Just the most expedient one.

You'll want to review our book on Green Water Strategy to gain more understanding of what is happening to you. You will also discover ways to stay afloat in these trying times. Meanwhile, abandon ship or move closer to the helm.

Frank and Willard

The iPod Of Management Techniques

Among other things, Veneer Management is a product of the new age of Marketing. Promoted by clever yet shallow managers as a solution to their own lack of competency, the adaptability of its techniques to a wide range of managerial shortcomings has caused it to spread more rapidly than the latest internet video. In championing their solution, VM-Managers followed the model developed by Steve Jobs who invented a product we did not really need, persuaded us to buy it at a price that defied logic and sold it in numbers that astounded common sense. Now we cannot do without it! Think of Tom Sawyer with his bucket of whitewash: the marketing principles are the same.

There are those who consider Veneer Management to be a least cost option, finding it to be both easier to implement and ultimately more agile. Assessing the benefits of the methodology, they compare the effort necessary to employ a snorkel versus scuba gear. Anyone can use a snorkel as it needs far less training and has the additional benefit of being less costly. The individual, being in shallow water, assumes less risk in a safe and more familiar environment. In the same way, VM introduces less risk for individuals and businesses by floating on the surface while avoiding the potential dangers of the "deep dive".

The only problem really addressed by this methodology was the need of certain individuals to minimize risk to their career by hiding their lack of knowledge, experience and ability. Taking the next logical step, they began to utilize those very faults to ride the Corporate Escalator to success. VM represents the means to accomplish this mission. It has met with such great success that it has spread its grasping tentacles throughout the corporate world.

Veneer Management: The Basics

Veneer Management is an operational extension of the Green Water Strategy. It is the day-to-day practice of a minimalistic philosophy that has allowed a legion of new managers to rise to power in complex environments while avoiding the need to learn and understand the pesky details of their businesses.

From this analysis the basic tenets of Veneer Management have developed. The obvious implication of the name points to a new, shallower perspective. A thin skin of process, a shallow layer of procedure, a gloss of statistics all with a coating of ornamental leadership and you have a lovely veneer that overlays the wood-chip core with the same appearance as a more expensive product.

At the forefront of the VM movement one will find a group of people we refer to as "Natural VM-Managers". In response to the information overload and wildly increased expectations of upper management, these people have quietly moved into positions of authority. Their rise to power comes as a result of exercising a set of principles based entirely on the ability to deliver the impression of success. We will say more about these people as we study VM, but keep in mind their ascendancy is largely based on their ability to deliver *perceptions*, not necessarily products or results.

VM can appear in two forms: Controlled and Uncontrolled. The Natural VM-Managers are the source of the uncontrolled form in that they are acting in an instinctive manner designed solely around the goal of self-preservation. Uncontrolled VM will appear sporadically in widely dispersed pockets across an organization. In this form, it is imperfectly followed and as a result fails nearly as often as it succeeds. Because it sprouts up randomly, it can produce havoc when it confronts non-VM projects and staff. The controlled form can be found where skilled and studied VM-Managers make choices based on a specifically desired outcome beyond simple self-preservation. This form flourishes in the presence of stringently applied models for reporting and presentation. Though commonly working in opposition, VM-Managers will take on the appearance of working in concert.

The central theme of the philosophy of Veneer Management revolves around the concept of "less is more." By that, we mean that the less effort and time expended the better. As we have already pointed out, the less depth required the less risk to the outcome. While this may sound overly superficial, that is in fact the whole idea - superficiality. It is all about delivering an *impression* of positivity without the risk of experiencing nitrogen narcosis from the "deep dive".

The most successful VM-Mangers are those who expend the least amount of effort. That includes effort in understanding the details of the work they are managing. In the details, as the old saying goes, lives the devil. It follows that by not allowing those details to overshadow more important things, like perceptions, the result will be more successes achieved and the devil will remain safely locked up. Even more importantly, by not being mired down in complexities, the astute VM-Manager will be in a position to declare success regardless of the actual state of affairs. By disallowing a burdensome collection of facts to muddy the waters, it is less likely that anyone can verify the outcome contrary to what the VM-Manager declares it to be.

The skills associated with either goal of VM-Survival or VM-Success derive from knowing "just enough" to be believable. This flies in the face of the business practices taught in contemporary management programs, which are filled with phrases about "details" and "depth". However, the inability of the ordinary person to absorb enough knowledge to know what is really going on with every item all the time, has created an opportunity for both the Natural and Trained VM-Manager to thrive. It is all about presentation. The VM-Manager is able to deliver a view that matches the expectations of the audience. The content of this view need not be correct or even true; it must just present an image that satisfies the desire to believe. There is an episode from the television show "Seinfeld" in which Jerry's friend George says, "Jerry, just remember, it's not a lie if you believe it."

The existence of these practices has been revealed and exploited in popular culture through television, movies and cartoons. We believe this book is the first real investigation of VM where the current wisdom has been collected into a single source. By exposing the hidden secrets of Veneer Management with hints on how to identify VM-Practices, you will start to recognize these activities on your own. The

18

effects of the shallow mindset will be apparent in every department, every function and every team in a business impacted by VM. For you to thrive in this new world you need to be alert to the existence of VM in your business.

A familiarity with the theories behind these practices will enable you to deal safely with the consequences of the uncontrolled introduction of VM as well as navigate through the shoals of the controlled form. All you will need to decide is how you wish to apply this knowledge. Either you can arm yourself for survival amidst the seeming chaos of a VM-Organization, or, if you are more ambitious, you can sharpen your Shallow Skill Set and learn how to leverage your VM-Knowledge to place you safely on the Up Escalator.

Veneer Management Arrives "Just in Time"

The premise underlying the Green Water Strategy is that by executing a shallow approach profits will be maximized and costs minimized and success can be attained. Individuals operating in a VM environment are focused on maintaining their personal standing (survival) or seeking career advancement (success). To do so they follow the principle of applying the least amount of effort as they cultivate an aura of competence, guide perceptions, champion opinions, kindle emotions and downplay uncomfortable facts.

VM takes the "just in time" concept made popular in manufacturing and alters it to the form "just enough". Using that construct, you can accurately interpret every plan, decision and action taken by business entities as well as individuals. We have taken to identifying various elements related to Veneer Management using the format VM-*add-something-here*. You will see this throughout the text whenever we refer to principles, activities or theories. This helps to identify those things to which we attach a VM-Personality.

By understanding the underlying principles of having "just enough" knowledge to be believable, "just enough" ambiguity to assure freedom of action and freedom from criticism, and "just enough" personal involvement to appear important, the world around the VM-Manager becomes immediately explainable and navigable.

We do not describe success for VM-Managers as climbing the "corporate ladder" as that implies strenuous effort on their part. Rather, it is a leisurely ride up what we call the "Corporate Escalator". Deciding when to step on or off is the maximum stressor.

Embracing failure as a means to success is the first step on the escalator. It is a key concept within VM-Program practices. The agile VM-Manager is flexible, adaptable and crafty. She is comfortable with uncertainty, using it to her advantage. The purpose of the VM-Manager is to secure a successful outcome from a doubtful situation. In this respect, the VM-Manager employs a variation of the thought experiment of quantum mechanics called "Schrodinger's Cat". The original experiment involved a cat in a steel box containing a device that might or might not activate and cause the cat to die within a specified period. To the outside observers, the cat was potentially both dead and alive due to the uncertainty of what occurred in the box. Had the device fired killing the cat or was the cat still alive? Poll a random set of observers and some will say dead, some will say alive, some will say neither or both - you will not truly know until you open the box. (No fair banging the box first.) Likewise, a project is in an indeterminate state of success or failure but can be jostled into one or the other through redefinition of the criteria of success. VM recognizes that in such ambiguity lies opportunity.

VM does not suggest a wholesale renovation of management practices. It is a recognition of the twenty-first century concept of "just enough" management for success. The concept is applicable to the operational aspects of management and not the number of managers or the number of layers of management, as VM frequently implies an increase in both. Rather, Veneer Management in an operational sense is like the reflective micro coating on your sunglasses or that new paint color brightening your old kitchen cabinets. It is thin but it certainly looks cool!

Management styles and processes are evolutionary but are still in need of a re-imagining. The view presented here of Veneer Management is an outgrowth of years of observation and experience gathered across many industries. It is both a philosophy and a style that can be used as a lens to examine and explain any business environment. It is the presentation of "just enough" facts to be plausible and useful to the budding VM-Manager. All that is needed is to have "just enough" intelligent sounding lingo to allow you to appear as though you actually know what is going on.

This book itself is an organic expression of the VM-Philosophy. A key element is stating and restating the obvious in as many different sounding ways as possible. In pouring over records of old projects, the early appearance of VM-Thinking can be discerned in the popular joke about the Department of Redundancy Department. While intended to be amusing, comments about this so-called "mythical" department have proven to be true. The repetitious repetition of forms, training sessions and endless meetings has led inexorably to the spread of VM. If we appear to repeat ourselves, it is because we intend to repeat ourselves.

So Tell Me Why I Care About Veneer Management

If you find yourself asking the question "Why do I care about Veneer Management in my life?" let us explain in the simplest terms how VM can affect anyone.

A VM-Manager – who could well be your boss – is interested in the *perception* of competence. The VM-Manager does as little as possible for as short a time as possible to produce only what is necessary to give a believable impression of progress. The typical VM-Manager always has an eye on the next job and the next promotion, and will rarely stay in her current position for more than two years. You, on the other hand, the supposed long-term employee, are left holding the bag.

VM-Managers are adept at manipulating information to manufacture a string of successful events in the face of evidence to the contrary. In this manner Veneer Management influences the decision making process. VM promotes irrational behaviors, as seen by those outside its circle, which somehow appear completely rational to insiders. A VM plan expresses a generalized perception of expectations rather than containing the specific elements to ensure that outcome. VM status reports emphasize flash over substance in a not-so-subtle effort at misdirection. VM strengthens the illusion of competence by avoiding the need to display mastery of complex details. The result is that VM-Managers gain influence beyond their merit.

Clearly, the focus of the twenty-first century is toward shallower, less complex interfaces between any product and the customer, let alone manager and employee. Consider the once ubiquitous VCR with its baffling programming instructions. It has largely been replaced by the cable-box with digital recorder – the DVR. This comes pre-loaded with TV schedules and selection modes that allow the user to operate it the first time. The most useful and successful products bury complexity within a simplistic or shallow user interface.

Whose Idea Was it to Adopt Veneer Management?

Old-timers will quickly recognize the description "analysis paralysis". This is a state where decision making comes to a halt through an excess of data. Too much data has the effect of masking the path to forward movement. Having too many choices frequently results in none being made. Such a condition is virtually inevitable considering the state of management science as expounded by business executives and government agencies. The push is always for more detail, and more investigation, for without that there is no belief that a properly informed decision can be made. This thinking has produced a U.S. Congress that is frequently unable to function, businesses that complain of being buried in regulation and employees whose careers seem frozen in amber.

In the face of growing complexity in technology, information, regulation, practices and procedures, decreased staffing, reduced funding and shortened time lines, managers find themselves forced into a mode of doing less with less and expecting better results. In response, Veneer Management is an organic survival mechanism found throughout every organization. It is only by applying VM that the overwhelmed manager can continue to promote the charade of his value to the company.

In the world of the "deep dive", the quantity of information can easily swamp your corporate career. As manager after manager succumbed to failure as a result of the aforementioned "analysis paralysis", those left standing were quick to learn that giving in to the temptation of presenting true and often unpleasant news resulted in an unhappy outcome. It was easy to see that if only an impression of success was delivered, a positive result was achieved.

As an organic construct, VM differs from the "deep dive" methodology. The latter was developed intentionally as "sound" business practice. Veneer Management took root on its own through the instinctive reactions of Natural VM-Managers. As this group sought to survive the onslaught of change in the business environment, they found ways to present an image of competence. As one manager observed the success of another, the techniques were adopted and replicated.

Before long, these crafty Natural VM-Managers were shipping joyous success stories up the chain of command to their like-minded managers. Project success was uniformly reported, statuses looked good and so did their annual performance evaluations. In this way, Veneer Management techniques began to spread naturally. Much like the invasive and highly successful plant kudzu, which continues to overwhelm all efforts to eradicate it, VM has grown and expanded as each successful VM-Activity evolved. New managers who adopted these techniques were rewarded and moved up the Corporate Escalator. They left in place direct reports who had already become Natural VM-Managers through the influences exerted by their successful bosses.

Thus, there are managers who have discovered these guiding VM-Principles for themselves and have employed them with differing levels of skill, intent and success. That is the puzzling aspect of Veneer Management. The untrained Veneer Manager may exhibit amusing behavior as if they had stepped out of a page from Hans Christian Andersen's fable, "The Emperor's New Clothes" or the obsessive behavior of the captain of the USS Caine, Lieutenant-Commander Queeg. The true aspect of Veneer Management lies somewhere in-between.

As we observed these mysterious activities, occasionally asking, "Why are we doing that?", or "Do we really need to include this?" it became apparent that this approach was often something most managers readily accepted. Either it was a classic case of "We've always done it this way" in which common sense was sacrificed as an element of project overhead, or it was a case of Veneer Management. That is, if I add just enough corporate speak and use the right acronyms in my communication, it will appear as if I know what I am doing. In colloquial terms, giving it a "lick and a promise" and sending it on its way. Later we learned this was a VM-Based Product – Making Work for Other People.

Ironically, the lure of the "deep dive" seems to persist even in the world of Veneer Management. Largely because of the longevity of the phrase, it has become a standard mantra to be issued at any time a decision seems either difficult or uncertain. Over time, the overuse of this phrase has so diluted its meaning that it is rarely executed upon any longer. In truth, hearing the call for another "deep dive" has come to mean the encoded order to do nothing, expect nothing and decide nothing. In that sense the deep dive has been transformed into the near-perfect VM-Concept since it avoids everything. It has become the tool of choice for deferment of all activity by shifting responsibility to an unnamed team and an unstated future date.

Through a close study of the principles outlined, any manager will be able to take on the protective coloring of Veneer Management to adapt to the new organizational ecology and to recognize other managers who are doing the same. Now about the secret handshake...

Veneer Management is Here to Stay

The pace of change in the digital age, particularly as associated with devices, is incredibly fast. The old need for planned obsolescence is superseded by the continual stream of inventions and improvements throughout every industry. This element alone has contributed to the deprecation of technical knowledge when selecting personnel for a management position.

Indeed, in the fast-paced world of the twenty-first century, the possession of knowledge may actually be a hindrance. The party of the "Know-Nothings" has been reborn. Further, when management takes on the patina of age, either through advancement in calendar years, or time in the position, changes are indicated. Such a situation is akin to shellac yellowing on plywood cabinets and the extent to which changes are applied will vary. There may be the occasional touch-up where an individual manager is replaced or a wholesale renovation in which entire departments are removed.

In any event, age and cost are often a consideration and the era of the skate-boarder cum manager is upon us. Veneer Management is both the acceptance of and the realization that the changes accompanying this revelation are now common business practices. In order for managers to succeed in this rapidly evolving environment, it is only necessary to have an elementary understanding of the procedures and processes needed to survive in the new business world. In actuality, simply having a nodding acquaintance may be enough.

Implementing the principles fostered by the Green Water Strategy through the application of Veneer Management, you can be assured that the latest and best tools are now available to you. While experience in the software development industry has supplied the major revelations of these principles, the application of Veneer Management has proven universal. These principles are found, applied in varying degrees of thinness, to all industries and at all levels of management, from the individual project and line managers to members of the executive ranks.

A Force for Good or Evil?

The world economy is teetering on the edge of calamity. Job markets continue to shrink and employment is neither secure nor certain. Wages are dropping worldwide. The housing market shows few signs of stabilizing while investments fluctuate like yo-yo's. Banks and investment firms continue to report massive losses, attributed to poor decision-making and lack of management oversight. Governments are paralyzed and going broke and the leaders of these governments are despised. This is a crucial time to bring the principles of Veneer Management to light.

Finding ourselves faced with inexplicable phenomena, we concocted a few organizational theories, some psychological models, a handful of rules of behavior and one or two operational methodologies as investigative tools. As part of the analysis, we added some arcane mathematical formulas as we attempted to make sense of corporate and government decision making.

The result is… we are not sure. Veneer Management saves time. It certainly saves effort. It can also save the VM-Manager from the disappointment of a career blocked or deflected by investing too much time and effort on steering a ship lost among the shoals. What we do know is we have proven the existence of this new methodology. We have strong evidence of its rapid acceptance and spread. What we do not have is enough performance data to determine the long-term outcome of VM and its effect – good or bad - on business and government.

In this book, we have given names to the many operational aspects that represent Green Water Strategy and Veneer Management. Activities and behaviors that represent these VM traits will continue to exist and operate into the future. Given the increasing pressure to reduce time and costs and seek the mythical "more with less" outcomes, these business practices are not likely to go away although you may come to know them by other names. Regardless of how you recognize them, for the individual contributor or the manager, an understanding of the workings of VM on contemporary organizations is an absolute requirement to avoid the unemployment line.

After a quick review of what we have covered in this chapter, it is time to discuss some of the more obvious features of Veneer Management. We will also look into some of the more negative behaviors and characteristics that appear in a VM Organization.

Summary

Veneer Management is a popular new methodology for business and government organizations. Calling it "Veneer" is an attempt to steer away from the cumbersome deep dive modalities that are popular in business today and pursue the "Shallow Solution" instead.

Natural VM-Managers provided the impetus in the growth of VM activities. As a successful means of protective coloration, they have been able to enter the corporate gene pool to spread their principles by manufacturing a demand for them. The Kraken patrolling the corporate ocean has now been identified. This book is the glass-bottom boat of managerial study through which you can safely observe the life forms just beneath the surface.

Having insights into the "how and why" of the modern corporate world will enable you to find the most secure ground on which to build or protect your career. Unearthing the hidden secrets of business and government practices will help you avoid the pitfalls that have trapped many of your uninformed predecessors. Understanding the concepts explained in this book will help you avoid or at least delay having the roof fall in on your corporate existence.

VM includes a broad-based set of theories and principles which the newly christened manager can learn to adopt to survive or succeed in the corporate world. She will be able to "hit the floor running" and inspire her team to ever greater success simply by being able to provide the appropriate corporate-speak phraseology we have all come to expect.

The VM-Manager can be assured that through careful application of the ideas presented here you will reach your end goal in less time and at a significant savings. After all, the less you do, the less it costs

WHY DUMB THINGS HAPPEN TO DUMB PEOPLE

Launching the Lifeboat

Dear Mr. Frank and Mr. Willard –

Lately a feeling of separation and detachment has come over me. I feel my sense of worth peeling away in a company where I've been a successful manager for many years. There is a growing gulf between myself, my peers and my superiors, a gap that I am at pains to explain.

I work for a large software company in the Western U.S. The company is very successful and continues to make money every quarter; but in spite of that, we have begun to experience layoffs. A recent reorganization placed the management team in new positions after which staff positions were cut. My team has lost some very senior people.

I do not understand these decisions by leadership. Project plans seem to come from nowhere with little or no relation to what our customers are asking for. Timelines are set before we get the assignments and yet my team is held accountable when dates are missed or product content falls short. Where are these decisions coming from? I have no idea what to do to get reattached.

Please help me.

Coming Unglued in Utah
==========
Dear CUU –

You have described the behavioral patterns consistent with what we call a "Veneer Management" organization produced by a widening separation between yourself and those who subscribe to this philosophy. Our caution is of course, "Mind the Gap". Unfortunately, the answers to your questions, which we hear from many others as well, are complex and not quickly answered. We do, however, have help for you.

Included is a copy of our book "Green Water Strategy" for your edification. Study the explanations and concepts in this book and you will (a) understand the business environment in which you work (b) learn to identify activities that are consistent with what we refer to as VM-Practices and (c) learn to position yourself and your team for either survival or success in this unsettling climate.

Since the glue is not sticking, hold securely to a handrail.

Frank and Willard

The Illusion of Competency

Each of us can call to mind a person who seems mismatched with their current job. The person may be a team member, a peer or even a boss. Examining the qualifications of these individuals does not reveal why they hold the particular position or what makes them qualified for it. At times it is not even clear just what it is they do. Sometimes the person is imposed from outside the organization and other times it may be a self-inflicted wound from a faulty candidate vetting practice. There must have been an indication of competency at some time, but you cannot imagine just what it was.

Seen through the lens of Veneer Management, the nature of competency takes on an appearance at odds with common sense. As with many other attributes such as the definition of "quality", "done" and "success", VM applies its own selective definition of what does and does not constitute competency. Without taking into account the VM slant, it becomes easy to observe individuals of questionable capability who thrive in spite of their lack of obvious skills. These people seem to be stealing their paychecks. And while they may represent the worst of what Veneer Management brings to the organization, they somehow seem to be the ones who are the most successful at it.

The pressure to display competency increases with the frenetic pace of change. Veneer Management begins to materialize as a result of this demand. Unlike the forces that create a diamond from carbon, the pressure in a VM Organization is likely to create little more than a cubic zirconium. It may have the appearance of a diamond, but under the microscope, it is simply glass parading as a gemstone.

As new technologies emerge, specialized skills are required for their application. A software engineer learning to use Java must absorb a basic level of knowledge and demonstrate a mastery of it in his coding assignments. A certain amount of objective evidence then exists through testing and peer reviews to expose the depth – or lack - of this mastery.

The manager, standing above the engineer on the Corporate Escalator, now needs in addition to project management skills, some idea about how to best utilize this new Java technology and the resource supporting it, as well as how to evaluate that team member's performance. This is difficult without an equivalent amount of training on the part of the manager. How can the manager judge the abilities of her team member without knowing the details of the work?

Today's managers must deal with the introduction of many new technologies and their proper application. The details of any tool, technology, process, and procedure flash by in rapid succession and with such speed, that mastery of any one of them beyond the moment is unlikely. In some ways, it is like learning to ski when each trip up the mountain is on a different hill and requires different equipment. Each lift ride drops the skier at the top of a new and unknown slope. Not having mastered the skis used on the last run, the skier is faced with different conditions, using new gear each time. At least on the mountain there is a Ski Patrol keeping an eye on wayward skiers.

The mass of administrative tools adds to this burden. From new phone systems to new email programs, version upgrades, time reporting, expense reports, performance evaluations and training systems, maintaining competency is a challenge and may be the least of your problems. Organizational changes imply new reporting requirements and create demands for new or different skill sets. The federal government or even one or more international organizations may want to get a piece of your flesh as well. In this climate of technological overload, is it any wonder people scream and pull their hair out, begging for relief?

Veneer Management responds: "Why bother?" The ability to show competency in the face of such overwhelming change is demonstrably not possible. In that case, attempting to do so is doomed to failure.

As a result, Veneer Management produces another basic tenet: "When you can't solve the problem at hand, redefine it as a problem you can solve". Mastery of the technological elements is thus excluded from the VM-Managers' repertoire.

Instead, the VM-Manager focuses on the necessary reporting skills to hone presentations and guide review sessions to the desired outcomes. Written and verbal communication skills become paramount in a constant personal management of the message. Competency is therefore redefined as the ability to collect and manipulate information to create the proper image of competency at a project level where the details are greatly summarized and the actual state is left to the imagination.

The Degrees of Stupidity

We identify Competency within VM as related to a Measure of Stupidity – The Degree of Stupidity (DOS). There are three Degrees of Stupidity:

DOS – Level 1 - Dumber than a stump but knows it
DOS – Level 2 - Dumber than a stump but does not know it
DOS – Level 3 - Does not know what a stump is

Interpreting competency in these terms produces the following table

Degree of Competence	Description
Competent	Knows what a stump is and how to create one
Competently Competent	Knows what a stump is and how to get someone else to create one
Competently Incompetent	Dumber than a stump but knows it
Incompetent	Recognizes a stump but mistakes it for a table
Incompetently Competent	Knows what a stump is but believes the stump fairy makes them
Incompetently Incompetent	Does not know what a stump is but is unaware he does not know

Some say that if you are incompetent you cannot know you are incompetent but we disagree. A person can be incompetent and know it. That is an example of a competent incompetent. An incompetent incompetent would be unaware of his incompetence and therefore be completely incompetent. When sitting at the conference table and the statement is made, "We don't know what we don't know," you are in the presence of a competently competent person. Conversely, when a statement such as, "That will never happen" is made, you have met the truly incompetent incompetent.

The Natural VM-Manager, a wild, free-range individual, untutored in the formal body of VM-Principles will recognize their own incompetency and attempt to shield themselves using raw VM-

Concepts. By pretending to be thinking outside the box, they are disguising the fact that they are stuck *inside* the box because they could not get the lid open. The well-trained and prepared VM-Manager will intentionally assume the slipcover of VM-Principles to mask any aura of incompetency they may possess.

The Cosmic Stupidity Cloud - A Natural Phenomenon

Unrelated to the native measures of stupidity and competence, there exists an external event that has the effect of modifying competency levels independent of base measures. It has been observed that the cognitive abilities of an entire set of people can vary as a result of a previously unidentified external agency, either all at once or by ones and twos. It is as if a dampening cloud has shrouded them affecting normal brain activity. This effect may be observed as a sudden shift of reasoning in those individuals as they exhibit something akin to the mass hysteria of a religious cult suddenly seized by some sort of "spirit". Unsuspecting individuals may wander into this sphere and be likewise influenced. Team members that once exhibited functional levels of competency and incompetency quickly move to a fully incompetent state under this influence.

Given the blanketing and irregular properties together with the mysterious appearance and subsequent dissipation of the field, the effect has been labeled the Cosmic Stupidity Cloud. The CSC appears and disappears without human initiation or intention. Fantasists describe it as though the planet had passed through a comet's tail. A similar concept was first postulated by author Poul Anderson (*Brain Wave*, 1953). Anderson envisioned a dampening field which persisted over millennia. As the field receded, human intelligence advanced in great strides. So it is with the CSC. Its arrival precedes a sudden degeneration of intelligent thought while its departure offers a release from a behavior that can only be described as irrational.

You have likely noted a series of illogical decisions emanating from your management team or project leadership. These may be otherwise sensible individuals who seem in this case to be making one irrational decision after another. Rather than assume they have suddenly gone "crazy", realize that you have witnessed the settling of the CSC in your neighborhood. Beware of getting too close as you will not even know when you too have been absorbed.

The intermittent nature of the CSC indicates that it is a localized phenomenon. It is unpredictable, like earthquakes. It is something to be accounted for and its appearance expected at random times. The VM-Manager must keep a weather eye out for movement of the CSC toward the project team at all times.

In the case of the Cosmic Stupidity Cloud, there is little that can be done to alter its influence once it settles over a group. Avoidance is the only sure protection.

The Bright Shiny Object Syndrome (BSOS)

Persons in a Veneer Management organization will often exhibit a set of behavioral characteristics, which collectively are described as the Bright Shiny Object Syndrome. This is classified as a "culture-bound" syndrome as there is no underlying biological cause for it.

The very name provides a clue as to the meaning of this behavior. If you have a cat, no doubt you have seen how much fun they can have with a shiny object attached to a long stick by a string. To amuse the cat, you simply swing the stick and watch as the toy on the end dances in front of the cat's eyes and lures him to jump and chase. It is nearly as much fun for the human as it is for the cat. The cat is fascinated by the movement and, in the nature of cats, pretends to hunt and pounce on its prey.

In a similar way, VM-Managers are frequently fascinated by the lure of shiny new tools and cutting-edge technology, distracting them from their current purpose. Sometimes this is an active pursuit on the part of the manager who scours journals and blogs for the latest techno-whiz gadget. At other times these objects clamor for attention just as the dancing toy does for the cat. The cat at least has an excuse as it turns to this amusement out of a near constant state of boredom. The VM-Manager may be bored but normally has a brain larger than a cat.

Those afflicted with BSOS demonstrate a marked inability to focus on a single concept, be it a product, methodology, or project plan, let alone hold to it. They shift rapidly from one concept to the next without following any implied directional change to its logical conclusion and ignoring all possible consequences. As decisions are made and then unmade, course corrections are altered or even reversed. The changes, particularly any impact to a project, are ignored as though the original condition did not exist.

VM-Managers will attempt to justify their mania by expressing a belief that attaching this shiny new gadget to the project or product will be an improvement in quality, a reduction in cost, an advantage in the market or all three. These items have sustained a fascination for the VM-Manager and are referred to as "management bling." In the software industry, pursuit of such items would be with the intent to improve performance or enable new functionality. Occasionally this works out, but more often, the items are of questionable utility. Because it is new and shiny, it gives the impression of a modern product, at least to the VM-Manager. Beware of the lipstick on the pig.

In the VM-Environment, BSOS can be exploited as either a VM-Survival or a VM-Success tactic. Faced with the inability to manipulate a status report, tossing out a bright shiny object will move the focus from the negative to the potential the object represents. Likewise by returning again and again to a discussion of this bright shiny object or introducing a different one each time, the VM-Manager will be assumed to be forward thinking and ready to take on any new advance.

There is no escape from Bright Shiny Object Syndrome. One can only hope to be inoculated against its susceptibility. The first injection comes with being aware of the problems created by this condition. Any time you are in a meeting and sense there are a great many words being tossed around that sound technical and contemporary but that have no meaning, be suspicious of an outbreak of BSOS. One of the real dangers of BSOS is the inevitability that management will announce a directional change while still in the middle of the Rio Grande, saying, "I want to be on that horse over there".

Bright Shiny Object Syndrome is a readily observable and identifiable behavior commonly seen in upper and executive level managers although nearly every position is susceptible. Every time a new and exciting opportunity comes into view, the person is distracted to the degree that a project, or at times even a program, is initiated without regard to current activities. It is important to understand the distinction between avoiding deep involvement and comprehension, and simply being distracted by the next fancy car that drives past. That is BSOS.

A final word about BSOS relates to the use of this phenomenon as a VM-Survival tool. By introducing distracting features and tools and technologies to a manager or co-worker afflicted with BSOS, one can effectively distract them from any current activity. This can be useful if misdirection serves to raise the sails for a cruise across the Green Water to survival.

Launching the Lifeboat

Dear Mr. Frank and Mr. Willard –

I seem trapped in some sort of information dead zone. My product people hand me documents with requirements I can't make heads or tails of. When I propose something, they are in turn baffled by my presentations. Everyone's lips seem to be moving, but there is nothing but white noise received on both sides. Can you explain what is happening?

Mystified in Milwaukee
==========
Dear Mysty –

You are suffering from the business world equivalent of the common cold, and like the common cold, there is no ready cure. All you can do is wait it out. The cause of your predicament is a fluctuating Optimal Idea Density (OID for short) combined with a high-level Cosmic Stupidity Cloud breakout. The Optimal Idea Density range is characterized by ideas that are easily understood by normal people. This combination is currently inoperable at your site. At the same time, we suspect that the Cosmic Stupidity Cloud has descended in your area to such a degree that all communications have been impaired and are in what we describe as "Threat Level Opaque", the most serious condition.

Consult our section on "The Optimal Idea Density Factor" for a more complete discussion. You have two options in the meantime. Keep floating on your back and ride it out until better ideas appear and the CSC begins to lift, or accept the opportunity this confusion presents and manipulate the condition to secure your own advancement.

Frank and Willard

VM Information Theory

Everyone has an expectation of increasing what they know through attending classes, reading books, conversing with others and by just figuring things out. Within any collection of people, there are some who appear to operate under a permanent Cosmic Stupidity Cloud. The members of this sub-group have the unfortunate effect of reducing the knowledge base of individuals with whom they come into contact. These persons possess negative information which when combined with the positive information of another person not only lowers the total knowledge between them, it subtracts knowledge from the person having positive information. Essentially, by absorbing data from an external source, the sum of what you know has been decreased.

This concept was identified a number of years ago by researchers at several European universities investigating quantum information theory. Just as the mathematics of quantum mechanics allows for travel backward in time, quantum information theory describes the existence of negative information or negative knowledge. In cases where you seemingly know too much, negative information spontaneously appears to cancel out the excess so that you know just what is necessary, or in the parlance of VM-Physics, you know just enough.

The risk in VM-Project Management is that now you and your team no longer know enough to continue the project. On the other hand, this may be a propitious moment to start a new project. The quantum researchers suggest that by absorbing negative information, reducing the current stock of knowledge, an individual now has capacity to learn more. This is akin to saying, "I had to forget my anniversary so I could remember how to program my phone."

These researchers also detailed a condition where the total knowledge is more that there is to know. The example would be an apparent violation of the Heisenberg Uncertainty Principle where the position and the motion of an electron are both known. This is referred to as a quantum "entanglement". If multiple persons with this same condition come into contact, negative information can be produced as a result of their interaction.

In the VM-Environment, this can take two forms. The first results in a dissemination of misinformation. The VM-Manager is frequently brought to task for things that have not happened, things that did occur but are believed not to have, and things that are thought to be occurring in the future yet are unplanned. The second form occurs when the result of the collision is not simply a reduction of positive information or an excess of negative information but an imaginary value. Under the influence of this condition, the conceptual knowledge of any project takes on an aura of unreality when described by and discussed with upper management.

In quantum information theory, "qubits" replaces the well-known "bits" of basic computer language. In a computer, a "bit" is always zero or one, but "qubits" are in an indeterminate state neither zero nor one, or both zero and one (see the previous description of "Schrodinger's Cat"). This concept lends itself to VM as the state of any VM-Project is undetermined until the final iteration is under way.

The Evident Information Horizon

VM-Information Theory employs set theory to postulate an environment in which knowledge takes two forms: Known and Unknown. Each form represents a subset of the total volume of both sets. Each has an irregular topography in that they press upon each other in complex shapes in at least four dimensions. Time is a factor which affects both sets causing them to expand and contract in opposition. The sets are not homogenous in that each can encompass large or small portions of the other.

The Evident Information Horizon (EIH) is inclusive of all that is known about a subject. It is "evident" because we know it. This content can be relative to a person or a group. The information includes data developed through personal experience, data obtained from third party sources and found to be accurate, and data derived intellectually from a combination of the two. This later represents the Unknown in an intermediate or transitional state commonly referred to as "theoretical" which transforms into the Known or returns to the Unknown through a process of demonstration and experimentation.

Information that is Unknown resides below the Evident Information Horizon. It is Unknown for as Donald Rumsfeld put it, "We don't know what we don't know." The horizon appears at the boundary of the Known set but it can also transect the Known set where pockets of the Unknown exist. A visual representation would appear more like a typical Escher drawing instead of a Mobius strip. Data below the horizon may remain stubbornly out of sight or may come briefly into view and then quickly recede.

The Known set is not always stable. As the Unknown cannot be wholly known, except through individual hubris, it can through sudden expansion, affect large portions of the Known set, pushing it below the horizon again. The random element of discovery is responsible for such dramatic transformations such as the revelation that the earth was not flat but round.

The Google-Web interface is a tool available to VM and others in business to seek out data below the EIH functioning as a portal into the realm of Unknown knowledge. Due to the topological convolutions of both sets, this will return data below the EIH (things you do not know) as well as data within the EIH (things you already know). Further, while the Unknown may enter the transitional state moving toward the Known in this manner, as it was not derived through direct intellectual action it requires greater levels of demonstrability before it does so.

Since this concept applies to the group as well as the individual, there is a fuzzy boundary along the EIH since some will know and some will not know any given thing. However, since the group "knows" it if any individual knows it, the Group EIH represents the sum of the Individual EIHs. The Google-Web represents the equalizing force since it can deliver information that is both internal and external to the Group EIH.

There is a relationship between the Evident Information Horizon and Veneer Management. When dealing with the Known information set, there is typically a group of persons within an organization recognized as the "experts" on any given topic. These experts operate from a level within the Known set because of their experience. The belief within VM that the Google-Web can replace this base knowledge results in supplanting the old guard experts with the readily available internet. Short-term budgets benefit, long-term success suffers.

A standard of measurement for the EIH is presently under discussion by a committee representing the Evident Information Environment International Organization (EIEIO).

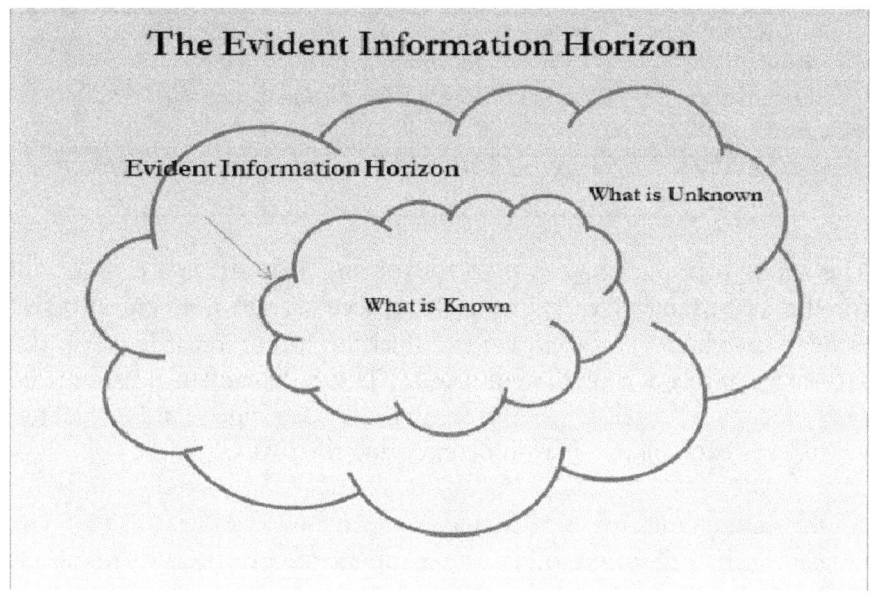

The Optimal Idea Density Factor

While many ideas sprout in the fertile minds of designers, users, salesmen, engineers and product specialists, few of them can be brought to fruition let alone survive the proposal stage. Successful innovations are not generated on demand. A new measure has been developed that will enable a prediction of success.

The Optimal Idea Density or OID is a measure of the complexity of any idea taking into account the communications required, written and verbal, the nature of the concepts surrounding it and the individuals presenting and receiving the idea.

Band	Rank	Applied to Concepts	Applied to Persons
Sub-Optimal Idea Density	Low	Devoid of Meaning	Simpleton
Optimal Idea Density	Optimal	Easily Understood	Normal
Super-Optimal Idea Density	High	Overly Complex	Incomprehensible

The ability to rapidly assess the OID of any proposal is a critical skill for the VM-Manager to cultivate. It is necessary to perform an OID evaluation whenever faced with a decision point regardless of the seeming significance of that decision. The independent attributes of the concept as well as the presenter are combined and evaluated together as each plays a part in determining the OID.

At the same time, the VM-Manager must consider the OID of any concept to be presented to his or her superiors. For the VM-Manager, in order to retain sufficient freedom of operation, the OID of any such concept or decision point must transition rapidly and frequently from the cusp on either side of the Optimal Band. This will ensure that each listener will have a different understanding of the proposal. The decision arrived at can be interpreted broadly so that any result is seen as a successful expression of the original proposal. Put another way, the VM-Manager must learn to use obfuscation as a way of life.

There is both an inverse and complementary relationship between the Optimal Idea Density value and the Cosmic Stupidity Cloud value.

The VM-Manager must be cognizant of the CSC and the potential effect according to the threat level it poses on both the decision-making process and the ability to actualize any specific proposal. The CSC has three measurements of risk – optimal, low and high. When combined with the three OID measurements this produces four benign combinations and five separate levels of threat to a project. The threat combinations are:

Low OID – High CSC (*Threat Level Maroon*)
When the OID is low or sub-optimal, the associated CSC value is high. This condition reflects the lack of conceptual references and the inability to observe or evaluate said condition. While mistaken for a steady-state condition, it is more often characterized by stagnation.

High OID – High CSC (*Threat Level Opaque*)
When the OID value is high, the associated CSC value is also high. This condition reflects an abundance of concepts but a corresponding lack of meaningful references for them. The presence of a high OID can spontaneously generate a high CSC.

Optimal OID – High CSC (*Threat Level Gray*)
When the OID is optimal, the high CSC can persist independent of the OID. It can dissipate but does at a rate dependent on where in the optimal range the OID lies.

Optimal OID – Optimal CSC (*Threat Level Pyrite*)
This is an oxymoron similar to military intelligence. There is no optimal value for the CSC other than a zero value, which is a measurement seldom if ever encountered.

Optimal OID – Low CSC (*Threat Level Dandelion*)
This is the ideal condition, which is unfortunately unstable. The OID will decay to the sub-optimal condition while the CSC will move toward the higher state. When this condition is observed to exist, all activities must be swiftly actualized to avoid the negative entropy of rapid OID decay. The rule to follow is thus Carpe Diem (seize the day).

Concepts may have high OID values without regard to their practical or impractical nature. As a result, the presence of a high OID is often associated with an onset of the Bright Shiny Object Syndrome. Items with a high OID and a low actualization value are said to have high AVOID value (Actualization Value Optimal Idea Density). Any project undertaken with a high AVOID value will quickly demonstrate the characteristics revealed in the V-Model (see "Fail Faster for Success").

The origin of the mortgage crisis is an example of a concept with a high OID value.

Conversely, Sponge Bob Square Pants represents an optimal OID value.

Persons with a high OID can fall into two categories:

> Those who produce concepts that collapse under their own weight (the Event Horizon Effect or EHE) or fail to reproduce (the Not Even Remotely Doable or NERD Effect)

> Those who generate concepts more quickly and more often than can be captured and realized (the Cheshire Cat Effect or CCE)

Steven Hawking is an example of a person with a high OID.

The Seattle Mariners management is a collective example of low OID.

Summary

The need to demonstrate competence is a necessary ability for survival as well as success in corporate life. The ever-increasing complexity of technical and business environments makes it virtually impossible to do so in a broad, comprehensive manner. VM-Managers have learned to demonstrate business-level competence through the manipulation of information and the manufacture of artifacts that present just enough facts to accomplish their aims.

Competency is further affected by levels of intelligence. Under Veneer Management, the focus is on the Degree of Stupidity manifested rather than of useful intelligence. Gauging the correct DOS of your staff, your peers and your bosses will identify which ones can be easily influenced by VM-Tactics. Those with real intelligence, who would have balked at this, have already left the organization.

The Cosmic Stupidity Cloud appears unpredictably to blanket persons in a random manner. It affects their ability to draw accurate conclusions from the facts or even to accept data as fact. Note that the arrival of the CSC can assist the VM-Manager making it easier to co-opt the team members into his alternate reality.

The Bright Shiny Object Syndrome frequently appears in organizations where Veneer Management has begun to dominate. Rather than rely on serious analysis of the value of new technologies and methodologies, executives leap at the opportunity to embrace cutting-edge ideas regardless of the cost or consequence. VM-Managers try to avoid contracting BSOS themselves; rather, they attempt to use it to their advantage by directing the attention of others where they wish it to be.

VM-Information Theory seeks to describe effects on the organization of the manipulation of information and its apparent value, independent of the CSC. It identifies situations where "the more you know, the less you know" and suggests that by absorbing sufficient amounts of negative information a mental "clean slate" can be established where the acquisition of new knowledge can be accelerated.

A measure of data contained within the Evident Information Horizon has yet to be defined. At a gross level, it is the sum of all knowledge about a particular topic possessed by an individual or a group. How this information is acquired, how it persists and changes over time influences the future of any business or project. The constant dynamic between the Known and Unknown is both a challenge to the VM-Manager and an opportunity to be exploited.

Understanding the idea of Optimal Idea Density can guide the VM-Manager to champion the right proposals couched in terms that will guarantee corporate support. Ideas falling in the middle band (Optimal) will routinely be more successful. Those landing on either side must be avoided. The presence of the CSC creates an increased risk or threat level to the VM-Managers' project. It is best to wait for it to recede before attempting anything new.

STAYING AFLOAT ON THE GREEN WATER

Launching the Lifeboat

Dear Mr. Frank and Mr. Willard –

I am at my wits end! My boss has just told me my team has to spend a full day tomorrow learning a new tool for submitting expense reports. This is after my team spent half a day doing a mock-audit of our time reports last week. Oh and by the way, one of the clients is expecting a promised fix a day earlier than planned. Which is good, my boss tells me, as the big boss wants to see the results of our IT study the day the client delivery was originally due.

We don't talk in terms of priorities here; no one ever says there are multiple number one priorities. These are not even stretch goals – they expect each one to be completed on time and on budget. I try to push back but get nowhere. Why can't she see the contradiction in these assignments? I feel like I've fallen into a George Orwell novel where facts are rewritten by the Ministry of Truth to fit each situation.

What can I do?

Perplexed in Portland
==========
Dear Perplexed -

One of the most difficult and puzzling experiences for all managers is to reconcile executive instructions that are obviously contradictory. Being able to live with such contradiction is a necessary trait in order to enter upper management. To explain this phenomenon, we developed The Principle of Divergent Convergence.

Giving teams assignments with identical priorities yet polar opposite goals is explained by this modality. Even when you point this out to management, the usual result is that regardless of the existence of conflict and in spite of schedule compromise, you must still "get it all done". Changes in timelines never accompany these new task assignments.

47

From the VM-Manager's perspective, it is all equally important. The ability to accept the concept of being in two places at once or of doing two things at once requires us to consider a possible explanation. Please consult our content in "Green Water Strategy" in the section on Divergent Convergence.

Recognizing that VM has arrived is the first step. Pull your lifejacket on snugly and use the red mouthpiece to inflate. That at least will keep your head above water while you locate the shore.

Frank and Willard

Veneer Management Bobs to the Surface

Like the red and white plastic float tied to your fishing line, VM floats on the surface of the corporate sea waiting for a nibble. As more Natural VM-Managers take the bait as part of their survival tactics, VM darts back and forth across the water. We are now detecting VM in the management styles and techniques of more and more individuals, though few if any of them are aware of its foundation in the Green Water Strategy.

Applying VM-Methodologies without forethought and perhaps without training is like throwing out your line for a bluefin tuna and hooking a great white shark instead. Gaining a surface layer appreciation of VM provides some insight to those Natural VM-Managers who are in a quandary about what is going on around them. Even though they are operating unaware of VM, their behavior indicates they have an aptitude for the shallow approach. However, unless they are part of a larger VM-Organization, surrounded by other knowledgeable VM adherents, it is best for them to maintain silence on the topic as a Shallow Thought proponent will find little sympathy from non-VM types who will likely consider such views either madness or heresy. Succinctly, the conclusion they will reach is that you do not really know what you are doing (though in the right context, that is a prerequisite for operating as a VM-Manager).

In this chapter, we will discuss some of the behaviors and activities that appear in a VM environment. It is important, while reading this information, to focus on the differing approaches related to VM-Survival or VM-Success and how they would be implemented in each of these areas. Much of the content of this chapter should be viewed as warnings against the inappropriate application of VM-Activities.

Playing a Round of Project Management Chicken

A few years ago, I was in charge of a large team made up of analysts and engineers. This group included a number of medical professionals with deep clinical knowledge. Our responsibility was to develop a component as part of an application destined for use in hospital settings. It would provide electronic assistance to the clinicians treating patients. The application was both critical in nature and highly complex – a combination that begged to be shrouded in Veneer Management.

Our specific component was tracked within a larger project plan, which monitored the development activities of many teams. All team schedules rolled up into the master schedule. Delivery was determined to be just prior to the end of the year. The work took place over many months with each team pursuing its own schedule and each team member responsible for his or her specific assignments. The abbreviated timeline was driven by customer promises and the inherent complexity and quantity of work made success a long shot. In spite of this, everyone involved strained to meet his or her deadlines. Separate from the project and also due at year-end were a number of mandatory training courses and the employees' self-evaluation. The teams believed there was only one obvious choice to make if the timeline was to be kept – delay the training and finish the evaluation work after the first of the year. Of course, that did not happen.

Just weeks before the promised completion and delivery of the application, the impact of Divergent Convergence was felt. Instead of making what seemed a logical decision, management delivered a mandate that everything would be completed by the required dates. Period. All training, all staff evaluations and all project assignments would be completed on schedule. Since all tasks were equally important in the eyes of the management staff, there would be no slippage on anything. There was clearly a belief that tasks could be added to an already full schedule without impact. This was certainly not the case. Ironically, the part of this plan that ended up failing was the client delivery. Training and evaluations were completed on time.

The Principle of Divergent Convergence

The Principle of Divergent Convergence defines the ability of an individual to maintain conceptual agreement with two distinctly dissimilar and logically antagonistic views. The term cognitive dissonance is at times confused with Divergent Convergence. With cognitive dissonance, the participant suffers from marked emotional discomfort regarding the conflicting views. No such discomfort is apparent with Divergent Convergence and in fact, the behavior allows the participant to believe both views are correct.

This requires the practitioner of Divergent Convergence to develop an internal explanation supporting the Postulate of Harmonious Recombination – a non-logical axiom in which these opposing views are, in some fashion, explained as either unrelated or, in the most egregious of cases, actually able to coexist in a new framework of reality that redefines the expected outcomes in an acceptable way.

Both the Principle of Divergent Convergence and the Postulate of Harmonious Recombination exist within a reality that is apparent only to the individual subscribing to the conflicting activities. It is always obvious to the outside observer that facts do not justify either the thought process behind such behavior or the expectation of the ability to support the naturally opposing perspectives.

It is necessary to consider the relationship between Divergent Convergence and the Bright Shiny Object Syndrome. Though a seemingly logical conundrum, the ability to employ these principles simultaneously demonstrates mental agility rather than mental impairment. Unfortunately, when combining the two, not only are competing ideas at play but random factors introduce faddish elements into the process. This has the odd effect of both working as a VM-Concept through the uncertainty and vagueness it produces, and at the same time undermining VM because of the added difficulty of delivering a convincing positive impression. Most baffling of all is the frequent occurrence of honors and awards being presented to those who seem adept at expostulating ideas combining this principle and the syndrome.

Success or Survival

Sir Isaac Newton, in developing his early theories of physics, believed it was impossible for an object to be in two places at once. This theory is generally accepted to be true for most matter, including people. Albert Einstein waffled a bit on the Quantum Physics front that posited the ability of sub-atomic particles to occupy two addresses simultaneously. He was first for it, then against it – flip-flopping in a manner somewhat similar to our modern day politicians. Regardless of the facts and theories of sub-atomic physics, expecting your team members to adhere to the laws of quantum mechanics is probably unrealistic. Hoping they can accomplish more than one thing at a time is really just that – hope – and will inevitably result in a failure of one or the other of these tasks and in most cases both.

The Principle of Divergent Convergence explains the behavior often exhibited by VM-Managers. It does not offer proof of either the failure or success of this particular VM-Thinking; it only explains the mindset of the individual expressing it. Neither does it offer any substantial comment on sub-atomic particle behavior.

As a student of VM-Theory, and irrespective of your intended use of this knowledge, either for VM-Success or for VM-Survival you need to be aware of this phenomenon. It is easy to detect since it manifests as an unmanageable workload of competing timelines. Early recognition of the impending arrival of Divergent-Convergence will arm the VM aware individual to coming schedule complexity. Depending on the individual's position – survival or success – options exist for dealing with the upcoming doom. One can apply the strategies discussed later in this book under "Be Near for Success – on Vacation for Failure". Early detection will allow for positioning to use either option.

The most that can be concluded from the discovery of this behavior is that as a VM-Manager you can use it to express additional progress. Simply add more tasks to the "to be done" list and disregard the complaints you may receive from your staff when they point out the obvious conflicts. Remember the directive, "Do it all". Other statements that may be tossed around by the VM-Manager to address the problems created by over commitment are things like - "There are 24 hours in a day" "You can work week-ends and holidays." "You can sleep when you're dead." Newton's and Einstein's theories notwithstanding, in modern VM-Environments proponents of Divergent Convergence believe not only that your staff can be in two places at once but they are able to accomplish twice as much in half the time.

Divergent convergence is a VM-Principle that is difficult for us to encourage. While it does have the ability to provide the VM-Manager with some evidence of progress, the undeniable facts will not support any sort of long-term success in maintaining the resultant workloads. The practical view is that it is unsustainable. However, in a fully functioning VM-Environment with the rapid change in management and the ability to redefine all elements on the fly, the application of Divergent Convergence allows the organization to push the inevitable collision with the ground into the future. At that distance, it becomes something the next manager or team or project will have to avoid.

We support and practice many of the VM-Concepts discussed in this book, but this is not one of them. The only application we have been able to discover is a short-term boost to the image of the VM Manager practicing Divergent Convergence. For a very brief time, there will appear to be progress, but the overloaded team and unrealistic schedule will eventually collapse. If the intention is VM-Success in a very short timeframe, such activity might be useful. On the other hand, if this behavior is initiated incorrectly, everyone will suffer – the VM-Manager, the team, the client and the company.

Complexity - A Consumer's View

I picked up a small electronic gadget the other day, a pedometer, to track the number of steps I take on a daily basis. The device, about the size of a large wristwatch face, had four buttons positioned around the edges, each button labeled as to function – on/off – start/stop. There was no question as to their intended use. As is typical for me, without looking for instructions, I started pushing buttons trying to puzzle out the right sequence of events to get the device underway. Pushing the buttons on my own, I never got the same results twice. After about ten-minutes I gave up and opened the directions that were included with the device. They came on a piece of paper folded into a square not much larger than a postage stamp, which opened into an eight by ten page of incomprehensible instructions. I tried to follow them. I consider myself reasonably intelligent, but the interwoven complexities of the sequence of button pushing needed to make this simple device work left me disgusted and clueless as to how to actually operate it.

Complexity - A Developer's View

There was a time early in my career as a software engineer when I worked for a small company that ran the first generation of cash machines – ATMs – and later the first set of point of sale terminals. It was a small, privately held company run by a man who can only be described as a benevolent dictator. He had his vision of how things should work and he told us how to do these things in no uncertain terms. If you did what he told you all was well. If not, well one of his favorite segments at the monthly company meetings started out with him saying "New way to get fired!" and then he would tell us why we no longer saw "John" in the office. This was a man after my own heart.

He would show up in my office with a legal pad and a blue Sharpie marker, proceed to draw a few diagrams on the yellow page, then say something like "get that coded" and then charge back to his office where he would collect money for selling what it was I had been directed to do. I did code these things, and he did sell them. Life there was simple. You had clear direction and defined goals. There was no needless overhead and we had a very simple reporting structure. It was me, my manager, and the boss. We got a lot of things done in a short period of time. The company made a small fortune and soon was scooped up by a huge multi-national run by a man who thought nothing of sending his own people to rescue employees who were taken hostage in foreign countries.

Complexity - A Manager's View

Most people will tell you that the development of complex products requires complex management. The question really is whether the management needs to be complicated or that the complexities need to be managed. In my latest position in the software industry, I had the opportunity to manage an interdisciplinary group of engineers charged with developing new features for a medical information system. I was a cog in a large organization just the same as my staff. I heard the same information from my bosses that they heard from me. We listened to the same blue-sky messages from the executives who never really seemed to be talking about or even to us. When I chanced to look at the number of management positions between the most junior member on the team and the chief officer of our division, I counted three times the number of slots compared to my first corporate experience. The difficulty of command and control in such an extended hierarchy cannot be underestimated.

Does It Really Need to be This Hard?

The careful VM-Student soon realizes there are many observable behaviors that indicate the presence of Veneer Management in your organization – or in your life. The prior pages detail many of the more common ones. We have discussed the puzzle of competing objectives, the mysterious distraction seen in VM-Managers and the mounting levels of complexity that have overtaken us all. The world of the "blue Sharpie" seems far behind us. Gone is the era of simple tools and simple solutions. The world of the "unusable pedometer", one populated by complex products with promises that cannot be delivered, is now dominant.

It is a fact that most things in our lives have grown more complex. Partly this is due to increasingly powerful technology. We make things more complex because we can. In some cases, this makes sense. The earliest home personal computer came with 64k of memory and an external tape drive that was little more than a cassette recorder. One could type a letter and then send it to a noisy dot-matrix printer that took about as long to print the letter as it did to type it in the first place. Today the processing power in your cell phone vastly exceeds that of those first home computers. The Kindle application on an Android device uses a little more than 13Mb – compared to the tiny memory of those earliest devices - and that is just one of many apps available on it. The increased complexity is a real boost to productivity and to convenience. It adds a lot to our lives. That is, unless it becomes entangled in VM.

The reality of discovering VM in your life or your business is that you are faced with an outcome seemingly contrary to the initial factors that caused VM to appear. The move to shield and avoid complexity, perpetrated by the original Natural VM-Managers has given rise to even more complexity. While struggling to shield incompetence and ineptitude while still delivering a message of success, the Natural VM-Managers have set the stage for more complex and poorly understood solutions.

Complexity - A Virtue, a Goal, an Obsession

The twenty-first century is a complex place. Computers are required to run everything. In fact, complexity is believed to be imperative: Adding value and utility *must* require complex solutions. The latest electronic games demonstrate Arthur C. Clarke's dictum, "Any sufficiently advanced technology is indistinguishable from magic." Everyone can be a magician in his or her own living room, a la Harry Potter.

The best products are produced using methodologies that support the KISS principle: Keep It Simple Stupid - first uttered by C. L. "Kelly" Johnson, the original team leader of the Lockheed Skunk Works. Whether applied to an airplane design, a political message, organizational hierarchies, or processes and procedures, the intent of the motto is obvious. As we have observed, the best products hide their complexity through a simplified or simplistic user interface.

The presence of needless complexity is a sign that VM has taken hold in a project or product. It is a routine matter for VM to overload a project in an attempt to raise the perception of increased utility, value and importance. Within the project, this is signaled by a sudden shift in requirements, design or technology. VM forces external to the project will also insert complexity in the form of new or revised standards and processes, new measurements or new tool sets. The cumulative effect of these alterations is generally opposite of the promoters' intention. Instead of improved and highly valued products, we find products swamped by gadgetry, bloated processes and procedures and communications choking on jargon. The functions may be there but no one can use them.

On the other hand, the VM-Manager must appear crucial to the project. There is no value in making the job look easy. If the task appears to be performed effortlessly, then the manager's role is either unimportant or can be filled by anyone. The prestige of a project and its manager are automatically enhanced through the addition of leading

55

edge technologies and complex methodologies. In doing so, the VM-Manager is recognized as making intelligent and critical contributions, which automatically increases her value to the company. She can offer the impression of proceeding in an intelligent manner and thus appear more valuable to the organization.

An unusable product like the pedometer is the result of applying uncontrolled VM-Principles. The wholesale addition of features or a complicated user interface confers on the VM-Manager a sense of responsiveness to market needs. Calling the changes a smart use of the technology places him at the leading edge. Ultimately, the purpose of a product becomes diluted and fails to achieve its original goals. The rule of thumb applied by VM-Managers is that "We haven't done our job if we haven't made it complicated."

Some VM-Managers might be described as technological groupies or junkies, depending on their level of addiction. Groupies are attracted to the "new" and "different" and exhibit symptoms of the Bright Shiny Object Syndrome. It is not necessary that these persons master the ideas let alone employ them in any manner. In fact, they may not be able to do so. They will pretend to expertise they do not have. Those who are even less knowledgeable will accept this pretense, when it is supported by a seemingly appropriate use of the terminology. The "groupie" is then labeled an "expert".

Technology junkies are fascinated by change. In fact, they are obsessed by it. The excitement generated by new products, new techniques, new methodologies claim the attention of these individuals to the point where they must have the latest version of everything. For these people the quest for new knowledge and skills is all-important. Theirs is a journey of discovery, which will never truly end. VM-Managers recognize this as it applies to project management. Asked when their project will end, they reply, "We're never done; we just stop working on it."

Considering the unusual and often fleeting applications that appear and disappear, the chief effect of these products is to demonstrate the slick use of new tools, new methodologies and new techniques. The management team appears to be at the forefront of technology while not risking their career in any meaningful way. It also infers a sense of market savvy, which is more often simply taking advantage of the obvious.

The Electronic Household

The faddish, trendy nature of commerce has an impact on products selected for development. A few years ago, it was mechanical kittens and puppies with the power of independent animation, tricks to entertain children while eliminating the care and feeding of real pets. This was soon reduced to a hand-held toy that not only simulated pets but people, too. From 1996 through 2010, 76 million Tamagotchi devices manufactured by Bandai were sold around the world. Not to leave adults out, the concept moved on to applications for your mobile device displaying animated figures that will talk to you and act in ways you can direct. Is this a child's toy or a moment's entertainment for an adult? What do these products tell us about the nature of society and family life in the United States and around the world? Do such products serve a purpose or were they created because they could be?

Name an electronic appliance and there is bound to be a product available with an imbedded computer chip. When added to wireless technology control of these devices, large and small, can be done remotely, instantly and as often as you like. Security packages exist that can turn lights on and off, monitor doors and windows and track who and what comes into and goes out of your house. A report of such activity can easily be made available. But, do you really need a computer to monitor what goes in and out of your refrigerator so it can send a shopping list to your phone or perhaps the local grocery to fill it like a prescription and deliver it based on your personal calendar for the week? Maybe your doctor wants to know how much butter you are using or is that 1% or 2% milk? The fridge could likely tell them.

Actually, some of this sounds pretty cool and if you were a fan of the Jetsons perhaps you have been looking forward to this. There is an associated risk with this increasing complexity beyond understanding how something works, whether or not is it useful or can even be done. The consequence of failure of a complex product such as your refrigerator or phone is much greater than that of your talking animal app. Introducing everyday products with complex technologies employing the VM surface layer approach to understanding consequences creates a questionable measure of reliability. The potential for cascading failure in that world is a disturbing prospect.

Is That A New Suit or Did You Just Get an MBA?

The full study of the historical roots of VM is outside the scope of this book. However, it is important to mention the significant effect on business conditions in the twenty-first century relative to some ideas that gained prominence between thirty and forty years ago. In particular, we mean the rise of the MBA.

In the late 1970's and early 1980's the MBA programs began to take on an allure for businesses and prospective students alike. Nixon's Wage Price Freeze and the oil embargo had cut into the profit margins and corporations were looking for ways to recover. Educational institutions saw the potential in such a demand, particularly for students already employed but looking for a means to enhance their corporate value. It was a marriage made in heaven. The corporations consented to pay for this education provided the student achieved an acceptable grade and made the initial tuition payments, which would be reimbursed after the fact, generally in place of a raise in pay.

From 1975 to 1995, the number of applicants for MBA programs doubled. The number further increased by at least fifty percent in the following years. All of these individuals have been schooled in the same principles, the same methodologies, and the same statistical models to produce a relatively uniform approach to business management across the board. In the service of their corporations, this has become an adherence to "the bottom line". It has also produced the idea that what it takes to manage one business is the same as any other. Hence, the principle of interchangeable managers has become easily supportable and widely accepted.

Things That Flourish Under Veneer Management

The MBA factories continue to produce members of that fraternity. The production of the MBA "product" has become a self-sustaining business. By stressing the importance of the bottom line and the need to manage costs, particularly labor costs, which mandates increased management oversight, the associated demand for managers has correspondingly risen. Coupled with the concept of span of control where limits are imposed on the number of direct reports rather than reporting levels, organizational hierarchies have ballooned in proportion. The introduction of dotted line reporting reflects the limitation imposed by describing the structure in a two-dimensional format.

More management is desired to ensure fewer failures, particularly in the areas of audits or lawsuits. More upwardly mobile managers with more potential slots above them means less time must be spent on substance and more on appearance.

Another business that has exploded is that of the process-improvement firm. These companies will help your business perform the analysis necessary, according to their particular methodology, to determine how to unleash the hidden potential. These organizations spend time with your staff helping collate facts and suggestions and prepare a report out to senior management at the end of the session. Though in great demand, it must be acknowledged that a consultant is merely someone who borrows your watch to tell you what time it is.

The application of Veneer Management is frequently an expression of vested interests protecting themselves. A prime example is the effort expended to define all entities, all practices and all measurements the same across a business. A pretense of equivalencies is maintained as outwardly the elements look the same when beneath the surface we find the well-known apples and oranges. Process changes are introduced to repackage other people's work while simultaneously shifting focus and responsibilities. Adding more change by introducing new technologies and organizational restructuring are desirable to maintain the appearance of forward progress.

However, operational change is frowned upon. There is a tendency to keep doing things the way they were always done. What is surprising is that the most beneficial changes are the least likely to occur. The overhead, the inertia, the corporate self-propagating life force makes operational change difficult if not impossible.

Launching the Lifeboat

Dear Mr. Frank and Mr. Willard –

Recently our company was acquired. The management team was sent to a weeklong training session from which they returned acting like a bunch of Stepford Wives. New process and procedure standards. have been introduced which are unrelated to what we do. Seasoned employees are shunted aside on make-work projects while newbies are handed tasks beyond their abilities. Time lines are getting shorter and cycles faster with little if any product created. On top of everything, a series of layoffs has reduced the staff to a bare minimum. Our new department manager has never worked in this field before and tells me that things will work out as long as we follow instructions. Clearly, standardization is an important productivity tool – I just can't figure out what we're producing anymore.

Baffled in Barstow
==========
Dear B.I. Barstow

Apparently, your enterprise is working toward the goal of doing less with less for less. Contrary to the old saw about many hands making light work, in your situation it is fewer hands making light of the work. Product was a twentieth century concept, particularly when associated with a physical object. In the new millennium, it is all about the process and the documents that describe it. Following the process is independent of the "product". Having identified a process that has been successful and extending it to every enterprise is a natural next step. It is sometimes referred to as the Law of the Instrument, which says loosely that when you have a hammer, everything looks like a nail.

Unfortunately, there is little you can do to alter this situation. You can review our section on the practice of the Unified Field Theory of Management to get a better handle on this trend. In many similar cases, the strategy has been to find the GAS Line and get behind it.

Frank-and-Willard

Unified Field Theory as a Management Technique

The study of management processes is often illustrated or emphasized by using metaphors and similes taken from athletics or the military. In most instances, the underlying theme is one of conflict with victory versus defeat a motivating factor. Our study found that the field of physics is an equally fertile one for offering new and different ways to think about the topic of business management. From Schrodinger's Cat to Heisenberg's Uncertainty Principle to Boyle's Law and Gaseous Diffusion, particularly related to the CSC, new ways of describing the business environment are invoked.

We now arrive at the Unified Field Theory, or alternately the Uniform Field Theory. In this context, the effort is focused on describing all relationships in identical terms with the goal of reducing everything to a single equality – in effect a singularity. In Veneer Management, this turns the astrophysicists' definition of that term on its head, attempting to achieve infinite volume with infinitesimal density.

A single explanation for everything is sought. One example is our use of the V-Model to describe all failure conditions. (See "Fail Faster for Success" later in this volume for details on this). Great effort is expended in creating scripts to anticipate and follow in any situation, in effect the creation of a Universal Playbook. If everything is uniform, then all functions can be optimized in one common way. Making software or plastic chairs or light bulbs or toothbrushes is all the same. Terminology is made uniform, as is training on all of the practices. If everything is identical, if everyone has access to and follows the identical materials, then identical results can be expected.

Having established this uniformity, it remains to produce staff to implement it. Some corporations are in the business of replicating managers then distributing them across every facet of their industry. Exporting managers to other companies through shared training, loaning them on assignment or strictly by changing employers, spreads these ideas like bird flu. Managers are trained in a common way of thinking, evaluating and acting independent of the line of business they will oversee. The VM-Manager is an interchangeable piece of the business strategy puzzle. Senior managers are given twenty-four to thirty-six month assignments in one business before being assigned to a completely different one with little opportunity to affect dramatic or lasting change. This seasoning of managers is an example of VM-Methods in its purest form.

Extending this uniformity to lower staff levels can be tricky, requiring an artful manipulation of assignments and project schedules. The basic approach to this technique lies in the initial selection of the staff. While multiple disciplines are represented in all projects, the premise is always that any member of that discipline is the equivalent of any other member. The institution of the pull system of work assignments mandates this approach. A judicious use of the iterative methodologies in vogue today further assists the VM-Manager in this pursuit. Any project shortfall remotely attributed to the staff resources can be redirected to a subsequent iteration. Even better, an instant redefinition of scope can move a problem to a future project.

Following this theory results in business practices and procedures that are the same; quality measures that are the same; staff members that are the same. It becomes the ultimate democratic approach and the end of the meritocracy – everyone is equal because we said so.

Defining the GAS Line

Frustration at work is a common emotion. Without regard to your job responsibility or position, events occur that leave you feeling powerless. Despite any attempts made to rectify a bad situation, the repeated inability to solve a problem eventually leaves one tangled with emotion, angry with most everyone and yelling loudly at the adjacent drivers of other cars on the freeway trip home.

In researching the emotional impacts of operating within a VM-Environment we uncovered an important concept that is both effective in combating this frustration and is easily deployed.

The individual suffering from VM induced frustration needs to be aware of two key concepts of the VM-World – the GAS Line and the Caring Curve. The GAS Line is a euphemism for the "Give a Shit Line". Using the acronym allows you to discuss this key VM-Concept in any company without fear of offending and risking a furthering of negative interaction that can lead to an increase in already mounting frustration levels. Related to it – The Caring Curve – is a measure by which we are able to track an individual's approach to the GAS Line.

Stated simply, as one's frustration level mounts it is important to recognize the symptoms and adopt a position of releasing your personal involvement with the events causing the frustration. By recognizing that your emotions are approaching a critical point, at which time you may be unable to edit your public comments, you will be able to detach and safely position yourself *behind* the GAS Line. Once you can acknowledge to yourself (and others if asked) that you no longer "give a shit" you will enjoy an immediate release of tension and find yourself able to function successfully.

The measure of your personal travels both in front of and behind the GAS Line is represented by the Caring Curve. As you more fully engage and increase your positive involvement with a project, your Caring Curve will move away from the GAS Line. As things deteriorate, you will be moving closer to the GAS Line as you prepare to step behind it. This topic will be covered further in the section "Managing Your Career" under the discussion on "Increase Your Productivity by Managing the CCI".

Summary

Natural VM-Managers increasingly use Veneer Management methodologies. This trend encourages other managers to do the same. A better appreciation of VM's integral nature with the Green Water Strategy will allow them to do so in a safe and secure manner.

The illogical behavior of upper management will frequently create a crisis where none existed before. The inability to prioritize beyond number one is neither a failure to choose nor a challenge to teams to improve. Rather it is a mode of thinking referred to as the Principle of Divergent Convergence. The mental parallel processing necessary to achieve this state commonly puts the manager on the fast track to success; however, the use of this principle will confound staff and court constant failure. Although you really cannot be in two places at once, Divergent Convergence allows an individual to envision a reality in which all things are possible.

Consumers, developers and managers each have their own perspective on the follies and foibles found in twenty-first century businesses. In each view, the common theme is the complex nature of management and how the objectives in a business can get lost in a muddle of process, forms, rules and hierarchy charts. After all, there is a reason why management is called "overhead."

A central objective of VM-Managers is to simplify and minimize the effort expended on managing any project, obscuring their activities in a psychedelic cloud of positive energy. Despite the intent, the outcome has been decidedly different. Practicing this art has made project management more complicated while providing less control and opening the door to greater and greater complexity.

The twenty-first century is complicated by the technology needed to produce important goods and services. People contribute by adding complexity to enhance their own value rather than the utility of the product. VM-Businesses exploit the faddish and fickle nature of the public. Regardless of the value, you can sell almost anything to anyone once. Having access to a large market, you can generate revenue by producing useless junk for as long as you care to operate.

Corporations are always looking for that white knight that will protect and maximize profits. In the final third of the last century, they found one in the holder of the MBA certificate. From that time on, these wizards have been held in great esteem. Producing such magicians is now a viable business on its own. Sister industries have been spawned in the form of consultant firms, which assist businesses to reach their goals through process and organizational improvements.

The introduction of the Unified Field Theory of Management applies the garment industry's "one size fits all" concept to all business practices. Extending the concept to staffing furthers the deprecation of knowledge and experience. Standardization equals increased profits because the MBA told us so.

Good mental health is a challenge when working in a corporate environment dominated by VM. Maintaining a personal perspective that places you behind the GAS line keeps a check on your mental and emotional stability.

FAIL FASTER FOR SUCCESS

A "successful failure'" describes exactly what 13 was - because it was a failure in its initial mission -- nothing had really been accomplished,"
> Jim Lovell - Commander Apollo 13

Launching the Lifeboat

Dear Mr. Frank and Mr. Willard –

I just got back from another company-wide meeting where the corporate mutual admiration society held center stage. One executive after the other congratulated themselves on a series of accomplishments that had little to do with my division's business or products. In fact, we are failing to meet sales projections, failing to keep customers happy and failing to admit to any failures. The only thing we do meet is an accelerated yet abbreviated production schedule that cranks out version after version with too little content and too quickly for clients to absorb.

Every new strategy, process and tool set that comes around has been championed by a series of revolving managers and twisted to fit our environment. A slew of PMP's, a host of black belts and an army of agile experts have come on board with little benefit.

I have to attend the meetings because if the audience is too small, these executives want to know why people are not attending and suspect we think they are not important enough for us to be there. At least they would be right about something. My impression is that the meetings represent just another item on their checklist of things they have to do. I don't see how this can continue and am worried about my future. What do I do?

Adrift in Albany
==========
Dear Adrift –

For a minute, I thought I knew you. It was not until you identified your location that I realized we did not work for the same company. Do we ever understand your predicament!

In Veneer Management, the usual strategy for manufacturing a positive outcome is simply to declare victory. We've seen an example of that when a recent President donned a flight jacket, stepped on board an aircraft carrier and proclaimed Victory! On that day, we learned that a Natural VM-Manager could change the state of world affairs simply by proclamation.

You are a victim of Veneer Management. By creating the appearance of progress and success, your leaders know they can keep their futures bright. Proclaiming victory, defining success by merely saying the words, they ensure their short-term survival. Early in our book, "Green Water Strategy", we offer the wisdom of George Costanza from Seinfeld who declared, "It's not a lie if you believe it". Study the section in our book about "Fail Faster for Success" and you will learn strategies for surviving, and excelling in this alternate reality.

Do not despair Adrift in Albany. You are not alone in the lifeboat. The survival kit in the boat contains food, water, and a flare gun. You get to decide which direction you point the gun.

Frank and Willard

Let's Talk About Failure

Projects fail for many reasons. Over the past few years the number of successes has risen, but the fact remains that most projects will fail. Some sink beneath the waves like the Titanic, horns blaring, lights flashing, smoke billowing everywhere. Others slip out of sight like a two man submarine with hardly a ripple.

When success is announced, it is possible that the project has actually completed. More often, it is through the use of carefully developed VM strategies that provide the "Sense of Success" rather than by actually finishing the planned work. For the VM-Manager, adoption of the principles leading to this "sense" is a core element of Veneer Management. Knowing how to manufacture the appearance of success in the face of failure is a critical skill to cultivate.

As the VM-Manager begins a project, the raven of failure sits on his shoulder. Any athlete is aware that you simply cannot make every basket you shoot or hit every pitch that is thrown. The VM-Manager must know how to remain above the organizational Mendoza Line, and learn how to make that .198 batting average appear as valuable as a .400 hitter.

This is accomplished through an understanding of the VM-Project Management and Reporting constructs. An incredible amount of failure can be hidden by inserting an appropriate level of misdirection. Through a methodology called "Aiming for Success" the VM-Manager can implement either the survival or success tactics. Turning a potential failure into success with just a few clicks of the mouse realizes the VM-Objective of Failure Viewed as Success.

Before the VM-Manager can begin practicing this art - how to multiply two negatives into a positive outcome - the elements contributing to project failure need to be examined. The VM-Manager needs to recognize failure when it appears and understand that no amount of planning will escape it. After becoming aware of these elements, every VM-Manager will be able to act according to the principle: "When you fail to fail, you succeed".

The V-Model - Describing Failure

The tools of modern program management include highly detailed project plans describing the tasks, resources and schedules necessary for a successful realization of the program goals. Yet many of these efforts end with a discernible chasm between the original intent and the final result. Commonly the program team fails to recognize this has occurred until the sales staff appears and tells the team, "I can't sell that!"

The well-prepared VM-Manager recognizes early on when this gap between the plan and the target begins to widen. The VM-Manager will sense immediately when the ship has drifted farther from land than the gangplank can reach. He or she will recognize that the plan simply will not support the remaining needs and only one outcome is to be expected. Though sailing in the shallow Green Water environment, any plan can still run aground while searching for the shore of success.

The more complicated the project the harder such drift is to discern. The project manager is inundated by large amounts of data. The coordination of staff assignments, scheduling, time reporting, and budgets can obscure the actual state of a project. Interpreting the condition of the project from such data is a bit like looking at a painting employing pointillism, challenging the observer to make something from many dabs of color or multitudes of data points. The closer one is to the picture the less visible the image. For a project manager swamped by volumes of data, the image is a blur at best.

A post-mortem on a project, or in the modern parlance retrospective analysis or simply "retro", will always reveal the existence of this gap, usually resulting in an "aha" moment of recognition. There is a temptation to attribute the failure to a series of irrational actions taken by a previously unsuspected and dimly viewed stealth agency. More commonly, it is a result of the hidden dynamics at work between parallel operations, which appear to be linked by the plan but in reality are driven by independent leadership with separate objectives. This can be the result of upper management placing their bets on multiple "horses", certain that one will win the race. Other times a decision is made to change "horses" in mid-stream. Causes may be found in the requirements, the design, technical choices, personnel assigned, or simply common misperceptions in any or all of these areas. In the end, it is obvious that "You can't get there from here."

Charting the course of the project, a gap appears between the initial goals and the final objectives. This is defined by a sharply descending line indicating progress forward but not toward the goal. At the point at which this condition is recognized, a sharply ascending line back to the objective is drawn to indicate the effort necessary to recover or "crawl-back" to the desired result. In the resulting figure, where the goals rest on the left tip and the objective on the right, we refer to this condition as the V-Model.

The V-Model can be used to describe any failure mode, large or small. In every situation there is a disconnect between intent and result. For example, the team members have a great thirst. They find themselves on one side of the Grand Canyon and the liquor store is on the opposite side. They just can't get there. The following page is an illustration of the V-Model.

Illustration: The V-Model

The 'V-Model' of Program Management

This is a visual description of the interaction between multiple, independent operations. Originally known as the Golden Spike Phenomenon*, this result is most often achieved when two or more initiatives are undertaken that, though complementary and integrated are driven by separate individuals, timelines, priorities and goals and without any effort at cross-communication. The effect of the CSC (Cosmic Stupidity Cloud) can not be underestimated. In the end, 'You can't get there from here'.

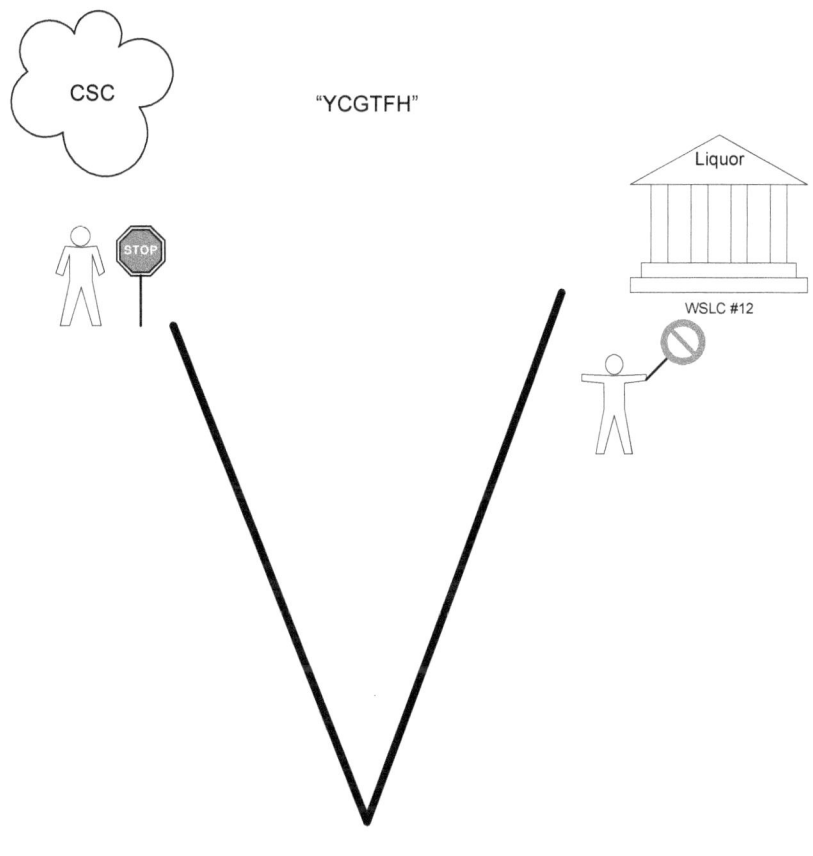

---

* The reference is to the meeting at Pikes Peak of the Union Pacific and Central Pacific Railroads. After covering considerable distance and at great effort, the tracks actually lined up and were the same guage.

The Futility of Planning - Proving VM Using Zeno's Paradox

A development project does not end until all requirements covered by the plan are complete. As the project proceeds and time passes, requirements are added which extends the project time line. The project is not complete until all the requirements are met. All requirements are not met or identified until the project is complete. Therefore, the project never completes. Under this scenario, all plans are doomed to failure. This is an illustration of Zeno's Paradox, which loosely says that before you can complete any journey you must go half the distance, then half the remaining distance then half again and again, never actually reaching the destination.

The explanation for this predicament in project planning can be borrowed from linguistics and the study of semantic drift. That is, how language, spelling and the meaning of words changes over time. Those of us who have had to read Chaucer in Olde English are familiar with the difficulties this presents. In VM-Project Management, it is related to the change in requirements from the Project Inception Point (PIP) or the Beginning of the Project (BOP) and the End of the Project (EOP). As the project moves forward in time, new requirements are discovered as well as changes in user expectations. This necessarily changes the purpose (or meaning) of the project.

Throughout the project, it is necessary to indicate a status, often in terms of percent complete, customarily represented by burn down charts. This status is calculated in terms of completed function points versus requirements plus user expectations. The result of this calculation should produce a measure of project completion in relation to the time remaining. We call this value the Not Quite There Factor. The formula is as follows:

$$NQTF = (CFP / (DR + UE)) * 100$$

In the equation CFP = Completed Function Points, DR = Defined Requirements and UE = User Expectations. To illustrate, a project was begun with 60 Defined Requirements and 30 User Expectations (sometimes called "delighters"). The following calculations of the

NQTF show the values at the beginning, middle and end of the project for CFP = 0, 45 and 90.

$$NQTF = (\ 0 \ / \ (60 + 30)\ ) * 100 = \quad 0.0$$
$$NQTF = (45 \ / \ (60 + 30)\ ) * 100 = \ 50.0$$
$$NQTF = (90 \ / \ (60 + 30)\ ) * 100 = 100.0$$

This factor indicates the completion ratio of things done to things to do assuming a steady state on the requirements front. However, over time, conditions change and the values in the divisor begin to change. New requirements are identified from internal and external sources. The longer the user community waits for a product the more their expectations grow, often spurred by the competition. Where the project once sat at a 50 NQTF, a 10% increase in DR and UE pushes the project back to an NQTF of 45.5. More often, this happens closer to the nominal EOP when the impact will be more pronounced.

All projects plans are subject to this drift. The VM-Manager can follow two obvious strategies. The first is a unilateral declaration that the project is complete. All remaining requirements are de-scoped and shifted to the next project. The second option is to plan for this inevitable situation by adopting an agile methodology. This involves the pre-definition of very short, successive iterations which can be completed before the changes to the requirements can affect the current increment. The effect of growing requirements and user expectations is only observable on the total project view and not the individual increments. The VM-Manager is able to report success after success for each succeeding increment. When this strategy is played out, he can then shift to option one and declare the project complete.

Calculating Project Drift

The project drift can be plotted over time. Two lines are drawn on XY axes where X is the NQTF and Y is the project time line. The first line marks the NQTF at succeeding points in time using the CFP value at that time and the original DR + UE value. The second line plots the NQTF using the same CFP value and the successive changed DR + UE summation at the same points in time. The distance between the two lines illustrates the drift.

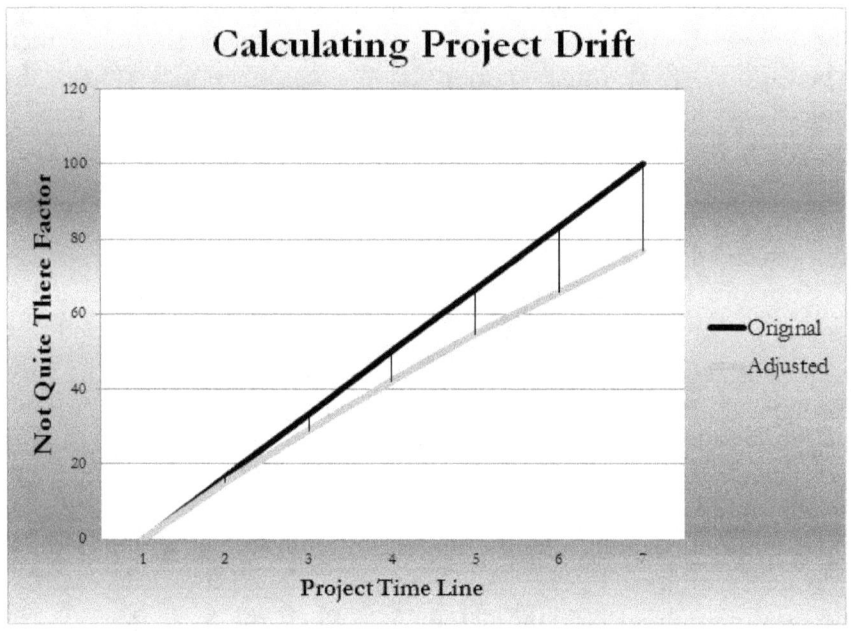

Failure Brings Success – Success Brings Failure

The VM-Manager is not afraid of failure, knowing that failure is always the first step on the journey to success. However, there is a danger in reporting a continual string of successes. This creates an atmosphere of increasing expectations, which automatically increases the VM-Manager's workload. Some of this can be delegated but given limited resources, failure is bound to occur. Eventually the load will exceed the VM-Manager's ability to perform, hence automatically sowing the seeds of failure.

Another aspect of this principle can be seen in The Law of Retrograde Productivity. This describes the state attained when one has achieved such a high degree of success that they have increased the expectations of others regarding their capabilities. This produces the unexpected result of the assignment of ever-increasing amounts of work until the point is reached that the individual is unable to perform to expectations. This state continues until failure is attained. A persistent condition of failure is often the result of random success – things eventually simply stop working.

The Case for a VM-Management Hierarchy

The after action report on a failed project regularly includes a multi-pronged critique where the tines point at three common causes. The first comes from executives who invariably determine that (1) more management oversight would have brought positive results. The rank and file point to the other two causes – (2) excessive management involvement or (3) the lack of management involvement. The only conclusion these groups agree on is that success would have been possible if the users or the clients had done a better job preparing for, and executing on their part in the now deceased project.

In order to address the first point on all future projects, more layers of management are added to the next program and the next project until the number of managers exceeds the number of persons actually performing the work. The organization chart describing the relationships becomes a maze of titles and roles with crisscrossing reporting lines, both dotted and direct. Navigating such a hierarchy makes it difficult if not impossible to identify the true decision makers. In fact, anyone on the chart with a sufficiently mysterious title can and will unmake any decision.

The addition of non-VM-Management Layers to address the perceived "Lack of Growth" (LOG) or to "develop improved measures" (DIM) and begin to "bolster up lagging business", together known as the DIMBULB approach, fails to produce results. Stacking layer upon layer of management in the belief that a better result can be achieved will have the opposite effect. Productivity is reduced, customer satisfaction is diminished, as are profits, and the business eventually incurs financial loss.

At this point The Law of Decelerating Returns has been invoked. This states that by adding more management into any organizational structure, the return on the expenditure of effort descends in the direction of the Zero Line. The Zero Line is defined as the point where the downward productivity trend has stopped and then becomes flat, neither rising above nor going below this threshold. This results in a condition where no positive or negative measurement is recorded. Time and effort are being spent but no movement – either up or down - is discernible. The project is not gaining ground, but it is not losing it either.

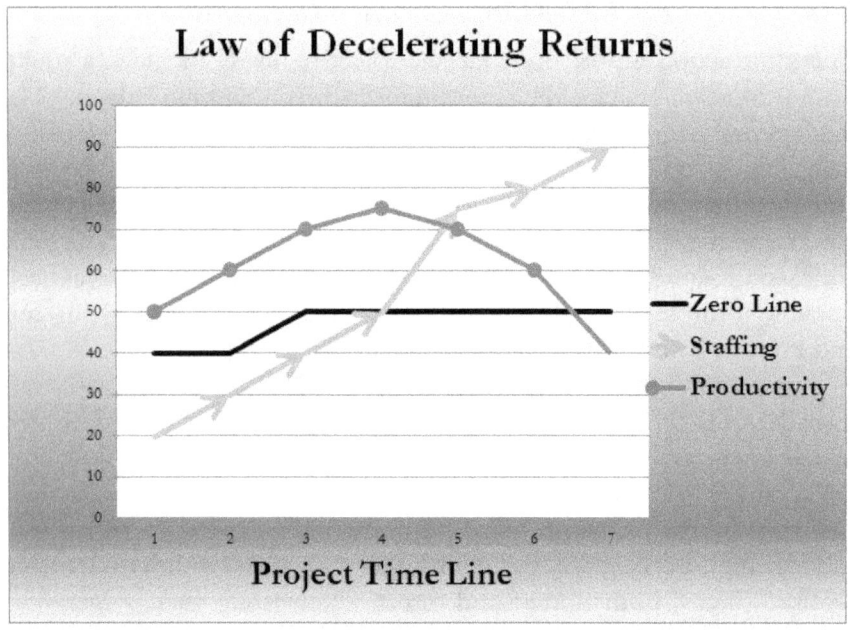

This is the danger zone because to the manager, all that is needed is the addition of staff to restart the positive climb. Theoretically, the addition of more resource has the potential of moving the measure away from the Zero Line. Actual practice has shown this to be a faulty expectation as expressed by Willard's First Rule of Software Engineering (see Appendix I), which states that adding staff makes everything take longer. There are instances where these measures can fall below the Zero Line. Events such as a wholesale revision to the project approach will effectively nullify all previous positive growth and send the measures spiraling down again.

VM-Management Theory leaves decisions about the depth of the organizational hierarchy to each individual business. To mitigate the impact of deep, multi-layered organizations, it stresses that VM-Management layers are thin, almost see-through like the Mylar you find as map overlays. Information passes through one layer to the next with minimal interdiction. The content is never obscured, only adjusted to the best advantage of each level's VM-Manager. As always, success is passed up the chain while blame goes down it. This approach breaks down in an environment overloaded with management layers, even in a fully actualized VM-Organization. There is simply too much water for sunlight to reach the ocean floor.

The Vegas Principle of Random Success

Everyone knows that if you toss a coin in the air there is a fifty-fifty chance of it coming up heads. With each flip, half the time we would see heads and half the time tails. Extending that to ten or a hundred times most people would say the ratio would continue to hold true. However, in an actual random system, flipping a coin ten times could conceivably produce heads ten times in a row. Just because the last result was heads does not guarantee the next will be tails.

In the same way, if one buys a lottery ticket week after week with the same numbers selected, eventually one will get a winner. The problem is, with the odds being some number of millions to one it is unlikely that there will ever be that big check. On the other hand, it could come up a winner the first day.

While tossing coins and buying lotto tickets are not generally accepted models on which to build business practices, the truth is a great many decisions are made based on the same pseudo-mathematical logic as shown in these examples. Simply put, if you do the same thing time after time it just might work often enough to convince you to keep at it. Winning a few bucks at a Las Vegas blackjack table will encourage the player to come back the next day, not to try her luck, but with the idea of building on the previous success. What this does not take into account is how all those giant casinos in Vegas were paid for in the first place.

In the business world of VM a great many managers play a version of blackjack when running projects. Having had success at one time or another with their specific choice of methodologies, they return to it again and again, convinced by the one or two previous successes that they know what they are doing. Each new project is undertaken with that same successful outcome in mind. This is the classic "If the only tool you have is a hammer, every problem looks like a nail". That is fine as long as all your problems are the same and turn out to be nails.

Success need come only often enough to draw the player back to the table. That is how the house wins. For the VM-Manager, it seems to be the case that given the general lack of knowledge and experience necessary to understand the long odds, it comes as a shock when the cards do not fall in the anticipated fashion.

Fail Faster with Process Improvements

In a perfect world, process improvements are expected to generate positive benefits. There is a process improvement subcategory, which supports the concept "fail faster" where the benefit is the reduction of costs by rapidly identifying wrong methods, wrong approaches and wrong choices. The first time we heard the phrase "fail faster" we were both a bit perplexed, but we soon learned that in the world of prototyping, finding a rapid failure point saves time and effort which means saving money.

This approach dovetails nicely into the overall Green Water Strategy by supporting an accepted view of doing less faster. By adopting the fail faster mode, the VM-Manager actually increases his or her chance of success if only by avoiding the unpleasant appearance of long hidden and costly mistakes. When operated under a sanctioned prototyping mindset, the rapid appearance of actual failures can be described by the VM-Manager as successes in the sense they have avoided a costly error that would only be discovered later. Again, failing to fail represents success.

We discussed the activities associated with the generation and adoption of ideas that are incorporated into organizationally mandated "improvements". Unfortunately, like so many things in the era of Veneer Management, the driving forces are frequently associated with the ongoing survival of the initiating agency much more than with actual improvements. Put another way, the group making the suggestion improves their chances of continued budgetary existence if the recommended improvement fosters the appearance of progress. This is an indication of an underlying VM-Motive.

When following the fail faster modality, the VM-Manager needs to be aware of avoiding the mistake of simply supporting her allied agency – the process improvement teams – by supplying them with ongoing short-term failures generated under the guise of progress. Eventually, her actual lack of progress will result in additional process improvement opportunities being exploited by the improvement groups as they add layer upon layer of well-intended "improvements" to the already faltering work. At some point, fail faster will morph into "fail completely" and the VM-Manager will find himself adrift with no lifejacket, no paddle and no hope. There is an additional aspect of process improvement that actually works in the favor of the VM-Manager.

Failure Hidden by the Screen of Improvement

We were surprised a few years ago when we realized VM-Managers had discovered the introduction of process improvements as a mechanism for controlling outcomes. New, unexpected activities were added to projects to create a project failure at will, or to disguise a pending failure. Labeling such an activity as "process improvement" commands a high degree of respect in the modern business and government environments allowing for its smooth addition to any plan.

The relative ease with which such activities take root in a project makes it easy to understand how it has become an effective means of scuttling a project. By adding additional overhead for training, implementation and reporting, a well-described "improvement" can cause icing on the wings of the project and the flight ends up against the side of a suddenly elevated process improvement mountain.

Paradoxically, it can also be used as a screen for the smart VM-Manager to cover an imminent failure. Adopting the attitude of "fail faster", adding a process improvement is advertised as a means for uncovering earlier mistakes. This serves as a deflection point for a VM-Manager caught with his pants down. By pointing to the inclusion of a new and improved process in the latest iteration of work, the VM-Manager can justifiably blame any failure point on a previously missed weak spot. Given a little time to create a suitable story, the VM-Manager can explain how a significant risk was uncovered as a result of inserting a new process, even when the process itself served as the trigger for that failure. Remembering the "it's all about perception" strategy, all that is required is a cleverly worded explanation to protect the guilty.

One of VM's governing principles is "the faster you fail, the closer you are to success".

Blind Reliance on Tools

In any discussion of failure as a product of VM, one topic frequently towers over all others. It is the belief that using tools somehow solves all problems. It feels at times as if VM-Managers hold a ceremony and issue incantations over the project plan expecting the magical appearance of automation to resolve all issues, both known and unknown. This belief, regardless of copious evidence to the contrary, is often regarded with a religious fervor in a fully operational VM-Environment.

Based on some long-forgotten successful implementation in a narrowly defined commercial product, a sort of magic has become associated with the utilization of non-human intervention. It may well be that following this single instance of a positive outcome, a budding Natural VM-Manager saw the injection of tools and automation as a plus since it enabled a furtherance of the VM-Myth. This unanticipated success because of the manager's obvious genius avoided the complication of actually using resources to complete the project. This approach supports a "tools as an alternative to people" strategy, which is popular with VM-Managers, as it reduces the time spent on human resource tasks. A smaller team means fewer hours spent talking to them. It also shrinks budgets, which makes all of the executives happy.

Another popular misuse of tools occurs as a response to the sudden appearance of a problem. Moving to a new tool or a new version of an existing tool in an attempt to avoid a project failure regularly courts that failure. The VM-Manager is able to deflect criticism by pointing to the active redirection of work from humans to tools and by offering evidence in support of automation. Should that not work out, a ready-made pool of culprits within the team is at hand to blame for not learning how to use the tools properly. The effect on the project is almost always negative and ignored. While the project team struggles to incorporate new or altered tools into an already overstressed timeline, the VM-Manager can include these alterations in the status reviews and enjoy the praise of his superiors for taking prompt and insightful action.

The authors do not categorically discount the use of tools. Certainly, we both understand and support the *appropriate* use of automation as a means to minimize effort and maximize quality. What we object to is the unfounded belief that all tools work for all situations all of the time. And that the insertion of a tool at any point in a project will produce positive results. This is clearly an overly simplistic interpretation of the value of automation, but it has unfortunately become a VM-Precept. You must expect to encounter it in any interaction with VM-Managers, and be prepared to find ways to absorb it in all VM-Activities. We have had many positive encounters with the application of tools over our careers. At the same time, we know all too well how a bad decision regarding tools can generate significant problems. One such example affected us both quite recently.

The Right Tool for the Job

Software development houses employ a multitude of "tools" for an almost equal number of purposes. Many take the form of utilities, which are native to the platform while others are additive components available from competing vendors. Choosing a utility involves factors such as features, cost, ease of implementation, training, support and the effect on the organization and in some cases on customers. Selecting certain utilities has potentially more impact than others due to the nature of the work they support. Tools such those used for issue tracking, test libraries and source control are examples of particularly risky areas. Changing a sensitive utility such as these can create significant concerns, resistance and animosity among their users. Such a situation came about in one business in which we worked. At various times all three of these tools were replaced. The one which caused the most unrest and concern was the source control system.

This utility had been in place for several decades and was commonly used by many other businesses operating on that same computer platform. Over time, it became deeply imbedded in the local processes employed by the development, support and deployment departments. There were known flaws and limitations and the chief complaint was that there was no graphical user interface or other "modern" features. In fact, a newer version of the utility did exist that met some of these objections but was not considered because of the cost.

It was finally determined that the existing source control system had to go. The reasoning behind this was never made clear let alone publicized. However, one specific feature was paramount: the desire to mechanically merge multiple development threads in-house and to do the same for deployment to existing customers. Several individuals were hired specifically to champion the effort and consultants were brought on to help design how the new system would be customized to the environment. The peculiarities of the source file organization, which had evolved over two decades, were at odds with the standard usage of the new utility. It was a case of fitting a square peg into a round hole. Eventually, with enough additional superstructures, the task was accomplished and the new source control system began to be populated.

Issues were raised immediately. Training was given to pilot groups who objected not to learning new methods but to the complexity of them and the fact that not all the features of the old system had been accounted for in the new system. The touted merge process would unpredictably produce a source file, which failed to build properly. Assumptions had been applied in conceiving the process, which conflicted with both the nature of the source and common practices. Concerns were expressed over source files which did build but would fail to function correctly or in ways that could not be detected until delivered to customers. In true VM fashion, the burden of proving or disproving the allegations was laid on the doubters rather than on the implementers. In the end, largely due to the incomprehensible complexity of the system, no smoking gun was found, just a lot of mini-firecrackers.

Because the mechanical merge process appeared to work so well, it became the accepted practice, which permitted a countless number development environments to spring up. Each existed for a different reason, contained different versions of common elements and persisted for widely different periods. The utility permitted a mapping of a file between environments and versions but the sheer numbers of them produced results that were beyond human comprehension. The results had to be taken on faith. Where the latest and greatest version existed was a matter of opinion. Consequently, all subsequent problem analysis stopped at the version in hand, as the genetic origins of the source were lost in the mists.

There is a post-script to the story. After having established the new utility and exported it to the client sites willing to accept it, it was determined to reduce the number of product lines and restrict further development for some undetermined time. Given the economic situation, sales had fallen off and competition had begun to take away existing customers. The need for the new utility began shrinking as rapidly as the economic fortunes of the business. The solution was, of course, to reduce staff snd the first to be released were the architects and champions behind the selection and implementation of the new source control system. The departments and the business sustained considerable churning and expense with unrealized benefits.

A true VM-Manager, particularly the Natural VM-Manager, will instinctively migrate toward tool utilization in every case. By attaching both a concept and a name to the tools involved in the project, the VM-Manager is able to deliver a perception of both knowledge and progress. Tools will invariably lead to a decrease in the number of staff required, giving the VM-Manager another medal for doing more with less, or in this case with fewer. And finally, the use of tools provides an effortless escape path in the event of failure. After all, if it operates completely out of view of the VM-Manager and everyone else, there can be no accountability when it fails.

Let's Build a Pet Rock - Defining the Proper Product

Why is it so hard to build something people want to use? VM pays attention to market demand in a search for economic gain. The rapid expansion of consumer electronics and communication devices opens the door to products such as cell phone applications, which are relatively inexpensive to build employing rapid development methods. For details on the approach Green Water Strategy takes on this concept, see "Micro-Segmented Marketing" in the *Green Water Strategy Manual* (GWSM).

VM also promotes the use of technological advances while giving a nod to advances in knowledge. Why is it then that so many projects end without a product or with one that is best used as a boat anchor, or with a little paint, one that can become a pet rock?

The addition of needless complexity has been highlighted as one reason this occurs. The question has to be addressed whether the unusable or unsalable product was the result of an intellectual exercise or an attempt to produce something of real value. In these cases, VM supports the generation of a prototype that begins as a demonstration and soon becomes the product. Because it was not completed or intended to be complete, it fails to satisfy the customer.

Another factor is the institutionalized process where a committee charged to build an elephant has produced a camel instead. VM follows a policy of inclusion where all interested parties are invited to contribute their views of what the product should contain. Actual experience in the field is not needed to participate. The requirement list expands like a child's balloon. Not every product can be the Swiss Army Knife in its field. It may have multiple functions but if it does none of them well, people will not use it. Checking off items from this massive to-do list may have satisfied the needs of the project sponsors but misses the mark where the customer is concerned.

Inviting customer input at the outset of the project is a valuable means of addressing this issue. This ensures that a relatively accurate picture is identified of market demand and the required functionality. VM has subscribed to this concept but will undermine the effort through selecting the participants according to its own needs. Selecting too few participants can narrow the focus while promoting a sense of partnership that does not truly exist. Conversely, selecting too many can overwhelm the project with competing requirements. The result may be a product without broad appeal or that satisfies no one.

The introduction of agile methodologies, the VM-Manager's friend, treats the problem of limiting customer input to the initial stages of the project. The purpose here is to ensure the project remains in synch with user expectations. This becomes a challenge for the VM-Manager to guide user expectations while manipulating the increments to manufacture success. The last thing any manager wants to have happen is to surprise the customer with a product that is vastly different from where the project started. The continual redefinition of the increments makes this a difficult but not insurmountable task for the VM-Manager. Defining smaller and smaller increments combined with a constant barrage of progress reports will muddy the waters sufficiently to obscure the true project course.

Consumer demand is a fickle creature. What was popular yesterday is so twenty-nine seconds ago. This is an ideal situation for VM: the unstable, rapidly changing product landscape is conducive to its intrinsic approaches. VM thrives because it never follows anything to its logical conclusion; it never does more than just enough to get by.

Particle Duality - Employing the Observer's Parallax Error

Those of us who have teen-age children have experienced the barely controlled anxiety of sitting in the passenger seat while teaching our sons and daughters to drive. As we check the driver's speed by looking at the gauge from that position, we shift from breathing fast to heart-pounding terror as the needle on the speedometer swings from left to right. The angle of this view never gives a true indication of the cars' speed as the parallax error introduced by looking at the gauge from this position may indicate the car is moving slower or faster than it actually is. The imaginary brake on the passenger floor gets a real workout.

Perspective also plays a part in evaluating a project. A manager needs to understand its state and status in order to make daily decisions. Sitting to the side in the passenger seat affects your view of the speedometer. Likewise, the organizational position of the observer affects their view of the project. Time and again, we have returned to the theme of duality – as in success or failure - in project management. Any project has elements which indicate failure or success right up to the final moment when the true state is declared. The closer you are to the project the more you see its faults and flaws as well as its gems, both rough and polished. The farther away the more you rely on previous experience to interpret the information you are given.

Despite the intention to create a condition where all things are knowable and predictable, hence subject to management control, projects have a way of slipping out from under the project manager's thumb. Just as an electron can exhibit both wave and particle properties, examining a project will find that failure or success is imminent depending on the observers' point of view or choice of measurement. The observer intends to apply objective measures to determine if a project is on course or not. Some observers collect details with which to measure percent completion to extrapolate the effort required to finish what is left, comparing that to the time remaining. Other individuals have their own formulas for selecting the indicators of success.

However, what the individual observer is viewing is variable and in the end subjective. The VM-Manager utilizes the format of the one-page summary presentation to manipulate and control the flow of information to the other observers. By focusing on positive trends, by underlining colorful events and highlighting exotic tools and technologies while downplaying mundane elements of scope creep and schedule changes, the report is assured of a warm reception. All the facts about a project are available if you wish to dig them out; but any conclusions reached and new decisions made are affected by this skewed perspective. Despite the facts, a belief is fostered that the project is on course.

As the true state of a project makes itself apparent to the VM-Manager, steps are then taken to reduce the status duality of failure or success and guide the result to a successful evaluation. New facts are marshaled, manipulated, colorized and condensed to present a new view of project reality. New phases or intervals appear as if they were always part of the plan. Scripts, dialogs and elevator speeches are prepared. The project status at the moment is declared and upon receipt of a consensual acknowledgement, returns to its indefinite state. The momentary crisis has been averted and the cycle begins again.

Launching the Lifeboat

Dear Mr. Frank and Mr. Willard –

Try though I may to comprehend what is driving decisions in my business, I keep coming to the same conclusion – I'm simply polishing the brass on the Titanic. I no longer see any outcome other than failure. And, no matter what the executives may call it, it is failure, not just a misunderstanding on my part.

It appears to me that projects simply end without warning and without meeting most of the original objectives. Am I mad? Or simply out of touch with reality?

Sincerely,
Seeing Icebergs in Indiana
==========
Dear Sailor –

Your problems may be attributable to the existence of a nearly invisible entity operating in your company in the same manner as seen with certain super-secret spy agencies in the government. While they may not have the same motives as the NSA or MI-5, they are just as difficult to detect and understand.

The Department of Intentional Failure is at work in your business. Their motivations and methods are as secret as their existence. While you will never be able to define the reasons behind their actions, you can certainly learn how to operate in the shadow cast by this agency.

In the section on "Exposing the Department of Intentional Failure" you will find an explanation for your troubles and advice on staying afloat amid the icebergs set adrift by the DIF. Keep a sharp watch on the sea ahead and avoid a collision.

Frank and Willard

Exposing the Department of Intentional Failure

During the early years of unknowingly doing research for this book, the authors began noting the frequency with which projects took on a new direction without prior warning or explanation. Work would be proceeding nicely with tasks completing on time and schedules met when suddenly the project would veer off course like an errant rocket reacting to self-destruct commands. And, exactly like that rocket, the once successful project would crash into the ocean.

Likewise, a project so off course that just coming to work had become an unpleasant experience would suddenly announce completion. Amidst the confused looks of the project team, grand celebrations would be held, promotions issued to those in the upper levels of the project team and honors bestowed on non-participants.

All efforts to understand and explain these puzzling and contrary events have revealed nothing conclusive. It is as if the operatives of a shadowy government organization are always a step ahead of us. Any evidence is concealed, the tapes erased, documents shredded or mislaid and persons assigned to different departments. The only possible approach to offering an explanation left to us was to concoct a theory - which of course we proceeded to do.

As we noted in the earlier discussion of failure, there is a natural inclination to seek agents responsible for these incomprehensible events. The working assumption is that someone or some group must want these outcomes, as there is no other rational explanation. As Sir Arthur Conan Doyle has Sherlock Holmes say, "Once you eliminate the impossible, whatever remains, no matter how improbable, must be the truth." Given this dictum, we have postulated the existence of a Department of Intentional Failure.

The following discussion of the Department of Intentional Failure is solely based on our theory of its existence, and on the circumstantial evidence supporting that theory. It may seem obvious that no real organization would actually field a department with the name "Intentional Failure". We recognize that corporations and governments can still shock us with their degree of arrogance and stupidity, but there is no record of any agency that uses this title. Whether such an organization exists or not, we have chosen to apply the name "Department of Intentional Failure" as an umbrella over the broad and varied events which separately or in concert undermine the efforts of hard working employees while simultaneously disguising the incompetents.

Under the Department of Intentional Failure Umbrella

It has been long assumed but never actually acknowledged, that all mid to large sized companies, and virtually all government agencies, expend a tremendous effort in Prevention Tactics. This effort is usually linked to Risk Identification and Management. While loosely accurate, it is not entirely true as there are purposes this group serves independent of the management of risk. For the VM-Manager, it is critical to recognize the nature of the activities initiated through this mysterious organization.

The existence of the Department of Intentional Failure, represented by DIF Teams, is known to a small set of executives but has on occasion come to the attention of VM-Managers. The teams and their members are usually unaware of each other. The opaque nature of these units is intentional. To mask the true view of executive decision-making processes and in order to achieve plausible deniability in the case of a large-scale failure, these teams must operate in the shadows.

Further, activation of the DIF Team may be for reasons that escape the comprehension of the VM-Manager and any rationalization behind these DIF activations will not be discoverable by them. The manager can only note that those actions have been initiated. For the purposes of this discourse, assume that the reasons behind the DIF actions are unknowable making it both pointless and unproductive to attempt to understand them.

The resultant DIF actions may be in direct conflict, not only with the project, but also with one another. Seen from the outside, a failed project looks like, well, a failed project. The inability to understand why this occurred is a natural outcome of the two primary and seemingly polarized functions of the DIF Team.

DIF Team Functions

The first function assigned to the DIF Team is to initiate a "Pure Failure". The purpose of a Pure Failure is to *cause* a project to fail through the initiation of any procedure, process or activity that will do so. Regardless of the means employed, a project will fail on command without recourse and despite any attempt by the affected team to recover the situation.

This is a key concept to grasp. The Department of Intentional Failure initiates the Pure Failure with the express intention of causing a project to fail. Under no circumstances will a project subjected to a Pure Failure NOT fail. Included in the DIF Teams' assignment is the management of that failure to completion *in spite of* any contrary intention of a person or persons not part of the DIF team. The outcome cannot be altered. The project will fail.

The second and seemingly contradictory function of the DIF Team is to implement a "Failure Failure." The typical driver behind this function is a need to maintain deniability in the event of an *actual* project failure, large or small. The purpose of the Failure Failure is to mask the reporting of the failure and thus the recognition that a project is in fact headed for the bottom of the ocean. One means of invoking this function of the DIF to eliminate the prospect of a dismal outcome, is by declaring victory: "My project did not fail because I said it did not fail."

Separate from these constructs is the actual "True Failure" condition. It is not an artifact and is not initiated or managed by the DIF. The True Failure represents a project that has, on its own, moved into a failure state or is at the Unconditional Failure Point – the UFP. The True Failure represents a self-generated or naturally occurring failure. The rest of the world will be aware of this. Detected in time, VM Management may be able to activate the DIF Team to begin Failure Failure operations. Other means are then employed defining failure as success. Here the Failure Failure function is initiated through obscuring activities such as the implementation of process changes, reporting structures and new tools and methodologies. This mode is termed a Shielding Action with the intent to avoid the blowback from a project True Failure. True Failures have a tendency to have an adverse impact on the projects executives and sponsors. It is possible for this operation to fall short of its goal. In that case, the true nature of the failure is not masked and blowback occurs.

These functions have been observed repeatedly over a number of years, but as mentioned, there remains a lack of information about the actual organizations behind them. While we see the evidence and the outcomes, we have yet to put a name or a face to the perpetrators. In spite of that, knowing the details of the activities that invariably appear as part of a DIF activation, we can offer direction for the VM-Manager to engage these groups.

Using the DIF to Your Advantage

Understanding the difference between the two DIF Failure modes offers flexibility to the executive sponsor or the VM-Manager. The Pure Failure allows a nearly completed project to be torpedoed and sunk while in sight of the harbor. The inability of the project team to comprehend what has happened allows an individual to alter the outcome of the project without having to invest in changing plans or later explaining why the project failed on its own. Being in control of the projects' fate through intentional failure, the VM-Manager can manufacture whatever story she needs to lay the blame on someone else.

The Failure Failure mode offers the ability to prevent the appearance of a project failure in reporting status. In this, the central VM-Principle, "If you don't fail you succeed" is paramount. By not allowing a project to fail, through implementation of the Failure Failure Shielding Action, the perceptive VM-Manager gets to present success in the face of what should have been failure. The failure was not disguised; rather the criteria of success was redefined or the cause was attributed to factors and persons outside the control of the VM-Manager

Managing Failure Is Hard Work

"This is the only project of its kind in the country, so I'd like to see it succeed,"
Deshmane said. "I wouldn't call it a failure, but it's not a success."
Whole Energy CEO Atul Deshmane

The activities taken under the auspices of the Department of Intentional Failure have a greater complexity than expected. It has been shown through anecdotal evidence and supported by informal studies that the effort required to engineer the perception of success exceeds the effort required to reach actual project completion by a wide margin. This is true for both Pure Failure and Failure Failure modes.

The challenge faced by the VM-Manager in dealing with the DIF is twofold:

First, the VM-Manager must be cognizant that DIF Team activities may be taking place outside her immediate area of visibility. Recognizing DIF activity is often difficult for managers, especially the experienced ones, because they tend to develop "project tunnel vision". These managers only focus on the specific goals of the project. They will become so fixated on the work that they will spend excessive time and energy, both their own and that of their teams on it, missing signs of a pending DIF intervention. For any project, there is always the potential for a parallel organization working independently to launch a Pure Failure plan; or for a project sponsor to pursue a Failure Failure option. The activation of either the Pure Failure or the Failure Failure scenarios may take the unwary manager by complete surprise.

The VM-Manager is most at risk in this situation as the probable target for any blowback resulting from the execution of these failure modes. Setting the operations in motion at the Executive Level, protecting the sponsor, or at the Project Level, protecting the authorizing VM-Manager, leaves the unprepared individual in the path of any potential consequences. Well-crafted Pure Failure plans will minimize this result; however, it has become the leading cause for transfers in low and mid-level management positions and the second leading cause for termination. Constant monitoring for suspected DIF Team activity is critical to both corporate survival and career success.

Second, the VM-Manager must be prepared to engage the DIF to initiate a personal Failure Failure plan. This plan should include a number of elements, chief among them several likely causes for the failure which were clearly not part of her responsibility or were out of her control. In addition a possible target or targets who might conceivably be blamed should be identified. This plan will need to be revised as conditions change and the project progresses requiring the VM-Managers constant and careful attention.

Activities Employed by the DIF
The VM-Manager must be able to identify DIF activities whether they are directed his way or not. The more common indications of DIF involvement include the following:

- Introduction of more granular levels of time tracking after project startup
- Scope changes that are initiated under the guise of client "must haves" or "fit for use" guidelines after project startup
- Introduction of new technologies: languages, hardware, data base utilities
- Insertion of priority client issues to pull team members from project work
- Sudden need for to complete training and unrelated to affected team member's job description and the project
- Creation of changed status reporting or tracking requirements associated with project, particularly newly identified Risk and Quality Management often attributed with governmental agencies
- Sudden interest in project from the executive sponsors

The DIF is in no way limited by this list or the elements it represents. Though a common misconception, it is sometimes assumed that the Cosmic Stupidity Cloud is a product of DIF origin. However, the Department of Intentional Failure Teams are equally subject to its influence with the paradoxical effect of making them more creative rather than less.

The penalty imposed through each of these DIF activities is that the extra work they require is never accompanied by relief in the schedule or by assigning more resources. On top of that, the team will be continually pressured by demands to complete on time or even early. These will appear under the guise of meeting "client commitments" and "market demands", or the risk of "potential job losses if we fail to deliver" and "failure to pass a federal audit." It is important for the VM-Manager to recognize these signs since they invariably point to the same end – this project *will be forced to fail*. By the time these symptoms appear a Failure Failure scenario may be already been designed and plans are being implemented to protect higher-level management through Shielding Actions. This would be a good time for the affected manager to consider reviewing the section on "Be Near for Success – on Vacation for Failure".

Anticipating DIF Activities

There are particular points in a project life cycle when activation of DIF teams may appear. The potential that a Pure Failure or Failure Failure mode might be undertaken on your project are at these times:

- You are behind schedule
- You are on schedule
- You are slightly ahead of schedule and feeling confident
- You bought a luxury car and/or just took out a new mortgage on your home.

The VM-Manager is adept at using failure modes to his or her advantage. Success is but one goal as the VM-Manager can make failure into a virtue as well as a success. With each failure, success is one step closer and the faster the failures can be generated the more quickly success will be attained. In the interim, the VM-Manager will be ready to snatch success from the DIF jaws of failure by judicious redefinition of the terms of success for the program. If the published goals are unattainable, if the product does not address the purpose for which it was originally conceived, take a page from the DIF manual and simply redefine the goals or redefine the purpose to ones the program actually does meet. By altering the definition of "done" the VM-Manager can always succeed.

The Dirty Little Secret of the DIF

We must point out an aspect of the Department of Intentional Failure that is often overlooked. We refer to this as "Ordering Takeout". While this might initially appear to be related to browsing the menu of your local Chinese restaurant while reaching for the phone to order the meal for tonight, it will not end with cracking open a fortune cookie. In this case, ordering takeout refers to the act of using the Pure Failure as a means to exact a price from another individual. It may be in response to some perceived slight to the initiator. It might be done to achieve career advancement by creating a failure for a competing co-worker. The resultant failure, exploited correctly, results in a positive outcome for the initiator at the expense of the target.

This is frequently the purpose when executive level managers initiate a Pure Failure. These are typically directed at a nearby peer in an effort to remove either an obstacle to higher advancement or a difficult co-executive. In this case, since the action is directed at a higher-level manager, the VM-Manager will remain untainted by the intentional project failure. At least this is true most of the time.

In the same way, it is possible for the DIF to employ an unsuspecting individual in a shadowy scheme of manipulation. The co-opted player will be operating on an agenda that differs dramatically from the secret plans being promoted by the DIF Team. The reasons for this matter less than the outcome. This frequently results in the unwary participant being blamed for an action to which she was not a party.

It is up to the perceptive VM-Manager to be aware of the possible activities of the Department of Intentional Failure and to ensure appropriate protective steps are taken. Like all agencies of business and government that operate in the shadows, the DIF can exhibit traits of the double agent when it suits their purposes.

DIF In A Nutshell

The Department of Intentional Failure operates on two failure modes in concert with or in opposition to an actual failure condition. The three types are:

- Pure Failure   – Initiated as an artifact rather than an event; will cause the project to fail
- Failure Failure – An artifact used to mask failure and provide protection to a select group; will prevent project failure
- True Failure   – An actual project failure which occurs without DIF involvement

The smoking gun for DIF activities is found when a previously well-conducted project simply goes "off the rails" with no definitive or discernible explanation. While these events often seem to originate as spontaneous project combustion, the thoughtful VM-Manager can, with a bit of investigation, uncover the sleight of hand that is the trademark of the Department of Intentional Failure.

Corporate history is replete with examples of projects that have been well considered, elegantly thought out, meticulously planned and yet for what appear to be incomprehensible reasons end in failure. There are times that these failures, coming on the heels of all the right planning are simply casualties of unexpected and dramatic market shifts. Examples would be property development projects put on indefinite hold following the banking crisis recently experienced around the world. Many public and private projects sit idle with the sudden disappearance of funding. Though often embarrassing and frequently financially catastrophic, these are not examples of activities perpetrated through the DIF Teams.

Summary

In the VM-World, all projects will appear to succeed. That is true even if they fail. By redefining of the term "failure", by crafting alternative views to project states and status, and by crafting data and reports to present a desired and positive image, the VM-Manager will produce a perception of success, even in the face of failure.

The V-Model is a graphical representation of the aphorism "You can't get there from here". As the implementation of VM spreads, it takes on the aspect of cold, hard truth.

Zeno's Paradox tells us we will never actually reach our goal. Before you can complete any journey, you must go half the distance, then half the remaining distance then half again and again. This explains why some VM projects never end. The reason for this is demonstrated through the calculation of Project Drift.

Management's response to failure is always to add more of its self. This is in conflict with The Law of Decelerating Returns as well as Willard's First Rule of Programming and is an example of Willard's Law of Retrograde Productivity. The downward path of progress is accelerated and prompts the question, "How many managers constitute a DIMBULB?"

One need only spend a few minutes on the Las Vegas strip to understand that the real winners there are not those who are putting their hard-earned money on the table. The clever operators of the cathedrals we call casinos understand and allow just enough winners to lure the players back to the tables. Likewise, in a VM-Environment, the occasional taste of victory is all that is required to ensure the engines will restart for the next project regardless of the outcome of the last.

Process improvements invariably produce overloads that naturally accompany their implementation. These frequently lead down the path to project failures. At the heart of VM is the idea that failure is a condition or state to be accepted and embraced as a necessary step towards success.

Tools and automation offer a tempting direction for the VM-Manager. By inserting automated and invisible steps in the project, either success or failure can be interpreted as success for the manager. If it fails, it is the fault of the tool builders. If it succeeds, it was a brilliant strategy on the part of the VM-Manager to include it. In true VM fashion, this ensures that all projects are successful.

Many projects fail to result in a marketable product. There are multiple reasons for this beginning with faulty market research, insufficient as well as hyper-focus on customer requirements and poor project planning and organization. VM works to mediate these faults in many ways, not necessarily to avoid failure but to ensure that the criticism of poor planning cannot be made. In many if not all VM-Projects, the artifacts become the product.

The VM-Manager uses concepts based on particle duality and parallax vision to allow the view from any angle to produce an understanding that matches the observer's preconceptions. This convenient bending of the light rays of project management ensures the VM-Manager the ability to deliver a perception that will delight the recipients.

While investigating the nature of failure we made a startling discovery. As in astrophysics where an invisible body or dark matter can be determined to exist by its effects on other bodies, so too have we identified the presence of a stealth agency seemingly dedicated to the generation of failure states. We have chosen to call this body the Department of Intentional Failure or DIF.

MANAGING PROJECTS

Launching the Lifeboat

Dear Mr. Frank and Mr. Willard –

I am a certified PMP and have the framed certificate and cancelled check to prove it. What I don't have is an unblemished string of successful projects with which to pad my resume. I've run out of clichés to describe my situation – I've got no creek, no paddles, no silver bullets, no golden parachutes and the future's so dim I've had to toss my shades. Although I've followed all the PMI precepts, developed well-crafted plans and paid attention to each and every detail, my projects are always blown off course.

Random elements crop up causing me to take evasive and corrective action until I can't steer my project back to port let alone find the dock.

What is happening to me? Am I cursed or affected by sunspots or global-warming?

Flailing in Fresno
==========
Dear Flailing –

There is a reason we have a section in our book titled "Managing VM Projects". You, my friend, are not the only one who senses that the ship has hit an iceberg and no matter how reassuring the captain tries to be, you understand how this is going to work out for you.

Project management and all of its accessory manifestations have become the loudest buzzwords of the current decade. A self-promoting set of organizations advertise themselves as the answer to all that is wrong with business, with America, heck, with the world! Next, we will be hearing we need to implement project management standards in our day-to-day lives to ensure we remember to take the dogs out and pick up the kids from school.

To all this, we say balderdash! This is a clear case of a good idea gone bad. The concepts you struggle to enforce in your PMP world are not wrong, they just require a different approach to work in a Veneer Management structure. The need for

97

detailed understanding is lost somewhere between the "let's go agile" group at the bottom and the "how much can we make this quarter" group at the top.

Study the concepts of VM-Project Management and perhaps we can shed some light on the things that are weighing you down and making it impossible to survive.

Frank and Willard

VM–Project Management

Veneer Management theory and techniques can be shown to apply to all phases of project management. In this section, we shall look at a number of phases of the Project Management life cycle in terms of their interaction with VM and offer you course corrections for those projects headed for the rocks.

Both of the authors have done a fair amount of project management in their careers. Some of that PM work was unintentional, because like many of the current topics and practices in business today, we had not yet adopted the concept of project management as a specific discipline when we first started our corporate adventure. Software houses introduced these practices in a formalized manner well after aerospace and defense industries. The truth is there was always some measure of "management" applied to our projects, even when we did not call them projects.

Many things failed or succeeded simply by accident, or sometimes due to inertia. Over time, and perhaps as a result of some spectacular, fiery failures, individuals began defining approaches that seemed the most likely to result in being able to complete what was intended. Over even more time, these approaches became practices and procedures and were eventually adopted as standards.

VM-PM - Certification

At the risk of imperiling my own Project Manager Certification – the coveted Project Management Professional Certification (PMP) – I have to question some aspects of this world. When viewed critically, the PMP and the Project Management Institute take on a similar form to the previously discussed MBA program. They are both self-replicating and self-serving entities, which profit mostly from their own existence.

The most apparent aspect of these organizations is that to be certified and allowed to wear the initials you must at the very least pass some set of tests. The PMP is not an inexpensive test costing between $405 and $555 depending on whether you are a member of the Project Management Institute. As of June 2011, there were 357,770 PMI members and nearly 438,000 active PMP certificate holders. The MBA? Well that cost dwarfs the price of entry for the PMP. Either way you have to admit, the awarding of these credentials generates a lot of cash for the granting entities.

Let us be perfectly clear about something before I completely obliterating any chance for us to work in the PM world again. The work that the Project Management Institute does, and the standards they promote and test for are all valid. This organization has, in fact, served as the model for the creation of our Veneer Management Institute. Likewise, things learned in MBA programs are valuable and useful. Like so much of what we discuss in VM, the ideas themselves are rarely the reason for why things go wrong, it is more about the subtle details of the administration of these ideas and their implementation into practice. Owning a car is not a bad idea. Driving it at a hundred miles an hour into a tree is. It is not the idea, but the implementation.

In the same way, having an MBA or PMP certification is most assuredly not a bad thing. We do have concerns about the Veneer Management perspective as it interprets the value of these credentials. There appears to be a VM induced belief that having either set of these initials after one's name (or even both sets) somehow makes that individual capable. The truth is it is just not that simple.

Credibility suffers, since for both the MBA and the PMP, the emphasis in business has shifted from seeking highly qualified, experienced and capable holders of these certificates to simply seeking holders of these certificates. This is not a result of either PMI or the universities selling MBA programs. For those seeking the certifications, there is the belief that adding these certifications will make them more money. This is usually the case. There may be issues when individuals seek these credentials solely for the purpose of increasing their income. The focus may shift from gaining knowledge to simply gaining certification. Less problematic is the pursuit of training for the express purpose of learning and increasing skill sets.

As we begin training individuals in the concepts of Green Water Strategy and Veneer Management and award Veneer Management Professional Certification, – the VMP – our focus will be on education and increased skill. As the VMP becomes a vehicle for increased income, we may well be faced with the same issue of having individuals seek the credential for strictly monetary reasons. As is the case with PMI, The goal of the Veneer Management Institute is education. See our appendix on the Veneer Management Institute for further details.

Hiring managers often miss acquiring true skill and experience in the rush to simply add staff with the appropriate credentials. The assignment of these three-initialed suffixes to names has resulted, in the VM-World, in an expectation of ability that is often not matched by results. Simplistically, the moral has always been "you can't tell a book by its cover". VM totally ignores that by taking certification at face value. If you are matching "credentials" to a list of positions with noted qualifications on a spreadsheet, you have done what was required.

Probably due to the effective marketing campaigns of the certification granting institutions, the perceived value of having the credentials has become much more important than having actual expertise. Thus, a VM-Manager will often assign credibility to his team based solely on the awarded credentials. It is much more difficult to explain the value of experience and knowledge associated with a team member than it is to merely point to their suffixes. In the VM reporting structure, as information travels up the chain of command, those titles give the impression of competence.

VM-PM - Walking the Walk and Talking the Talk

Many years ago, when I was working to get my private pilot's license I faced the step of having to pass a written exam before I was allowed to take my flight test with an FAA examiner. This makes good sense. There are many details to be aware of before positioning oneself several thousand feet above the ground. These include knowledge about rules and regulations, how an airplane works, how to navigate and communicate and much more. I not only wanted to be able to pass the exam so I could get my license, I truly wanted to know this information since it would be my backside sitting in the seat behind the controls of the airplane. It also meant I would be in that seat should the airplane encounter anything hard and immovable because of my own lack of skill or knowledge. Not knowing everything allowed for the possibility of immediate and unpleasant repercussions. I studied and I studied hard. Then I signed up for a weekend-long cram course in which I sat in a classroom for two days and heard everything I was going to be tested on for the written exam discussed repeatedly. At the end of the second day, on Sunday evening, after taking many practice exams, I took the actual test and passed it with a 97%. In this case, I like to think I actually knew the material, but the real focus for this "intensive course" was to pass the exam.

Last summer I sat for the PMP exam after going through a similar exercise. In my case, this came on the heels of six months of attending classes and detailed study of the concepts supported by PMI. I did the same thing as I had done for my pilot's license and attended an intensive weeklong study class. The truth is I knew the material for this test as well. However, if one really wants to pass the PMP, all that is needed is to shell out a few bucks to attend one of the prep courses and you will pass regardless of whether you really understand the material or not. Exactly like when I took my FAA test, I could have passed without really knowing the details of the subject. All I needed to do was sit through the class. The school offering this specific training even went so far as to guarantee my success. The obvious difference between these two scenarios is the potential risk of passing the exam without really understanding the information. You mess up in your airplane and you find out just how hard granite is. You mess up with a project and the worst that happens is you are asked to leave a job. The best outcome after an unpleasant result would be receiving a promotion. That would be a true VM outcome. The MBA programs obviously do not allow such a short cut.

The point of all this is quite simple. Having the PMP has become the new standard certification in the business world. It is the MBA credential of the new millennium. It is unfortunate that behind the acquisition of this credential is a growing industry designed solely to support the acquisition of the title and generate profit. The larger result of all this, in typical VM fashion, is the potential insertion of a project

101

manager onto a project simply because of the title. Experience has lost traction in the quest for the appearance of competence.

VM-PM - Begin with the End in Mind

PMI establishes a collection of process groups that help define the different areas of project management – initiation, planning, execution, monitoring, controlling and closing. By defining these groups one can break down the process of project management into small enough components to, at least superficially, simplify the work. Like most things in the world of Veneer Management though, this does not really simplify anything, it just makes it easier to present the appearance of being in control of the project. The first of these groups involves project initiation.

In the modern world of project management, it is widely agreed that a good starting point is in defining the work you want to accomplish. This is not only helpful in deciding what it is you want to do, but it allows numerous opportunities for the rapid allocation of blame once the project fails. This flies directly in the face of the "blue sharpie" model we discussed earlier because in those long past days the entire task of project management was reduced to a single page of legal pad – sometimes two pages for the more complex projects. Clearly, there were many problems with that approach. The obvious advantage of the old-fashioned "quick start" project was that it got underway very rapidly. Unfortunately, it usually ended in much the same fashion. Thus was born the concept of developing a charter and a project plan.

Like most of the PMI good ideas, in the VM-World this step has seen a number of unpleasant outcomes. Early in the process is the definition of the charter. A sample of the things one would expect to find in the charter would be:

- Scope
- General and specific objectives
- Constraints and assumptions
- Project organization
- Sponsor
- Project managers
- User representatives

- Technical leads
- Information on staffing, budget, communications, planning, tracking, change control, documentation, project plans and support information

Instead of the expected clarity of project definition and the hoped for positive results, the initial plan in a VM-Business will typically generate a hidden agenda that promotes things such as:

- Doing more with less – keep the team size tiny and the information output large
- Minimal effort equates to maximum gain – spend little and produce big
- Lower costs mean greater profit – define minimal costs in the charter
- Do nothing to reap the full profit – spend no money and all income is profit
- The less effort invested the greater the budgetary success – it looks good on paper

Essentially, it seems that most of the intention of a true VM generated charter can be viewed as the anti-Puritan work ethic – to do as little as possible but look good doing it. One of the benefits of well-crafted VM-Plan is the ready-made blame factor. Since the work is well defined, the timeline agreed upon and the staffing levels pre-expected, the inevitable failure of the project can easily be laid at the feet of (a) the incompetent team members, (b) the project manager, or (c) whatever other individual becomes the target once the VM-Manager sees failure as the only option. See the earlier section in this book dealing with the Department of Intentional Failure for more details of this fascinating area of VM-PM.

VM-PM - Let's Plan Our Exit

If you are fighting a war, or battling a wildfire in the mountains, there is no way you would dispatch a group of troops or firefighters without having a plan in place to get them out if things were to go wrong. Given that things seem to go wrong at least as often as they go right, it is not really an option but a requirement to have a viable exit strategy.

There is a general impression that through the application of PMI guidance a project will naturally work out in the end. As long as we track progress very closely then everything will be just dandy. Life is filled with examples of things that do not go right even though we watch them carefully. Your investment accounts, for instance. Or our politicians. Just keeping an eye on things is not enough. A continually updated action plan is required.

While a positive implementation of PMI Principles would seem to be the approach to take for successful execution of a project, the Natural VM-Manager has learned to expect failure at any point and spends much time quietly defining the work in such a way as to ensure exit options at all the right moments. While adding details that will allow for the appearance of effort, the actual purpose of much of this information is to serve as protection doing an early exit from the project. Much as a wild-land firefighter is trained in the deployment of their emergency shelter in the event of a burn-over, the VM-Manager plants exit signs along the project path to direct him to safety at the appropriate point in the failure process. In addition to pointing the way out for the VM-Manager, this can also work in the favor of the sponsoring executive regardless of the outcome. Failure never sticks to a VM-Manager. Even when there is an actual looming fact of failure, they are able to divert attention in such a way as to leave a successful impression. As part of this, a significant level of planning provides the appearance of work well done and will ensure a degree of safety for the sponsor.

After all, when so much time and energy has been invested in creating the collection of documents, which are stored in difficult to access and hard to understand automated systems, it is pointless to argue that the project was not well thought out. At this point, we are reminded of Charlie Brown saying, "How can we lose when we are so sincere?" If it is possible to trace the intentions to expectations, it can be considered proof that the planning step was successful A key element in recognizing a VM-PM-Planning activity is the existence of large quantities of documentation, even if, (and particularly if), much of the documentation is boilerplate retrieved from earlier failed projects. It must be clearly understood by the student of VM-Processes that the point here is quantity not quality. It really does not matter what you say as long as you say a lot.

An additional activity in support of VM-PM-Planning is the existence of a complex and convoluted approval processes, requiring review and agreement by a large numbers of people. The less directly associated with the project these people are, the more successful will be the appearance of proper planning and preparation. Additionally, the more approval points defined for a given project, the greater the opportunity for shifting blame.

A well-planned VM-Project will provide large quantities of documentation and a large number of emergency exits.

VM-PM - Let's stop talking about it and start doing it

The majority of VM-Project-Management activities occur during the execution phase. What that actually means is that the work on the project, whatever that may be, is being done. This can be confusing for the VM-Student. On the surface, this would appear to be the time when a product is created. This could be a software package being designed and written, an airplane being assembled, or an unusable pedometer being built. The VM perspective of this overlooks the actual *product* involved and focuses instead on the need to deliver the *appearance of progress* rather than actual physical progress. So to the VM-Manager, the execution phase is the point at which the appearance of a product or progress is generated. To the rest of the world, the belief is that a physical output will appear from this stage.

Remember that within the VM-Environment, it always comes down to giving the appearance of a result rather than creating a physical result. This stage of VM-PM is the central point at which nothing is actually produced except for the *perception* of something being produced. And remember, the more things created to generate the sense of progress, the better. So more status reports, more meetings, more schedules – it all adds up to the same opportunity to promote an appearance that may or may not be factual. If all this status information is actually backed up by a physical product, then the project can be viewed as a true success. However, if there is nothing but air behind the perceived success, it will be essentially impossible to tell the difference when only examining the artifacts.

The Execution Phase is a key point in the VM-Process in which the greatest numbers of people that will ever be involved in the project are actively engaged. This is the busiest phase, the time in which the most activity or perception of activity occurs, and most importantly, the time during which the VM-Manager will be most vulnerable to detection by the well-trained VM-Observer. It is noteworthy that during this phase, the creation of perceptions of progress will be accompanied by numerous documents demonstrating adherence to due diligence. Careful planning, careful tracking and continual creation of documented "proof" serve to inoculate the VM-Manager from wrongdoing.

This phase also brings into play the unanticipated appearance of players not listed on the team roster. Since no rule exists that one must provide a list of participating players prior to the game, the sudden arrival of a horde of unknowns can come as a surprise to the untutored VM-Manager. During the execution phase, a number of activities will require review sessions to gain full approval and support. At these review sessions, one should expect new participants to suddenly feel the need to insert their comments, whether appropriate or even correct, in what is usually a bid for acknowledgement. This may part of someone's personal VM-Survival or Success tactic but the impact will be felt by those attempting to move the actual work ahead. Awareness of this will allow the VM-Manger to at least anticipate this activity and rather than be caught off guard, they can prepare themselves for necessary deflection and restatement of any "issues" brought to light by the interlopers.

VM-PM - Who is Minding the Store?

Because you are now aware of the existence of VM, and in particular VM-PM, you will be able to discern certain activities which make visible the hand of the VM-Manager. In every project there will be processes implemented that define reporting activities. This step is designed to preplan the frequency and content of reports and will offer the sponsors and executives visibility into the project activities. It also serves as a means for the VM-Manager to identify and recognize when their ability to succeed is threatened. It is something of a paradox that the intentional insertion of complexities into these projects allows the VM-Manager to identify failure or success quickly based on being able to recognize having reached their own Point of Incompetence. We call this event the Point of Incompetence Trigger – the PIT. At the time the VM-Manager realizes they have lost the ability to pretend to know the details of the project, the PIT has been reached. It is time for the VM-Manger to act to save their career.

Preplanning a failure exit strategy during the initial project definition, and then creating a web of confusion around the mass of detail in the documentation, the VM-Manager can redefine success at any point simply by measuring current project performance against his own PIT. Put more simply, once the VM-Manager realizes she can no longer uphold the appearance of having any idea what is going on they can press to modify the plan to allow for success. This can be by declaring victory at whatever point has been reached and shifting the balance of the work to another phase (and likely another project manager) or by exploring the possibility of mimicking a Department of Intentional Failure event by generating blame on external factors.

VM-PM - Is That the End?

By definition, there is no such thing as an unsuccessful VM-Project. Regardless of the outcome, regardless of whether the intended product appears or disappears, or even ends up as some half-baked freak with small resemblance to the original plan, a well-crafted VM-Project will always appear to be successful. A project that either fails miserably and undeniably, or one that succeeds to expectations, will not have come from a VM-Business. The iPod was not a VM-Project. The success was absolute. The response to hurricane Katrina was not a VM-Project. The failure was absolute. The end of United States involvement in the Iraq War is an example of a VM-Project. Victory was declared in the face of dismal failure.

The key point here is this - the outcome of a VM-Project will be a success. Period. This is accomplished, if necessary, by redefining failure in terms of "success". This may be done by redefining the objective such that the end result equals success. Or, as in the case of a certain war, simply by proclamation.

The determination of when a VM-PM-Project is done lies entirely in the hands of the VM-Manager. Completion will be determined solely by the perception in the broader community. One of the more confusing aspects of the whole VM-PM-Universe is the complete lack of a quality definition of "done". It can be "done" either when it is done – the iPod again being the example – or it can be "done" when victory is declared as on the USS Lincoln. Unfortunately, these two views are not the only ones.

A more common declaration of completion comes when the VM-Manager, realizing that some critical point has arrived, will deem the work to be "done" simply because it is more convenient to their immediate needs than to any other requirements. This area defies predictability and means that you, as the hopeful survivor or success story in all of this, can only respond after the fact. At some point in your career, assuming it has not already happened to you (multiple times) you will suddenly realize that the project you are feverishly working on has completed without you being aware of it. Celebrations will be held, press releases issued, executive bonuses paid out and you will be sitting there with your fingers on the keyboard, ready to take the next step to completion only to realize they finished without you. The only response you can have at this point is to quietly shut down your computer, tidy up your desk and take a few days off.

VM-PM - Inertia - Applying it to VM-PM

One of the fundamental laws of physics is that of inertia. This was a concept cooked up by Isaac Newton and outlined in a book published in 1687. Having been around for such a long time, few people now would consider disputing the law, which essentially relates to physical objects and their tendency to maintain their current state. In other words, a rock you brought home from that visit to Crater Lake that you have on display on your desk will just sit there. Not moving. It likes that stability and unless you do something to change things, or there is an earthquake, the rock will most likely stay put.

Similarly, if you toss that rock out the window it will try to stay in motion in a more or less straight line unless acted upon by some external force – say the sidewalk or some poor pedestrian's head. In either event, the rock will continue moving – its current state – until an external force changes things. That is inertia.

It may surprise you to learn that inertia also plays an important role in VM-PM activities. There are legions of projects that have failed or succeeded simply through inertia. Once a project is named, it remains inert like the rock sitting on the desk. The challenge is to get things moving to the point that some form of VM induced perception of progress can be presented. Similarly, once underway and in motion – whether real or perceived motion – the project seems to take on a life of its own due solely to the effect of inertia.

Riding With the Tide of Inertia - Project Startup

The trickiest part of managing the inertial effects experienced by your project will be in differentiating between startup – riding with the tide – or completion – going against the tide. In both cases, your behavior will depend on whether you are student of VM-Survival or VM-Success. Regardless of the direction your boat is traveling, you can certainly learn to take the appropriate side steps based solely on the recognition of when inertia needs to shift. We refer this point as the Inertial Determinate Point.

At the outset of a project, when you and the project team are struggling to get the project into motion, your activities for success or survival are essentially identical. During this early period, you need to be a vocal attendee of all planning meetings, making certain the key project leadership recognizes your value based on an appropriate sprinkling of acronym-laden meeting-speak. At this stage of the project, the majority of the VM-Project Management team will be searching for a foothold around their still undefined individual Point of Incompetence and the more you say the better. You will know you have successfully established your credibility if you hear them repeating your acronymic utterances, particularly if you have cleverly inserted several meaningless phrases along the way.

At the point when your project team begins parroting your nonsense, you know you have reached a critical juncture and have arrived at the Inertial Determinate Point. The project is about to move. This is the time at which you will need to define how you wish to proceed. Will it be VM-Survival or VM-Success? You will alter your behavior according to those goals.

VM-Survival

The team, the sponsor, and the project manager now all believe you to be one of the most knowledgeable members of the group given your successful vocalization at the early meetings. Inertia is about to shift and the project will start moving, partially as a result of your inputs. Now you must quietly retreat, ensuring you have been assigned specific tasks that will enable you to sit on the sidelines and begin generating documentation for the use of the project team in whatever ways they see fit.

Removing yourself from meetings when possible is a good idea. It is easy to beg off given your specific skills and the need to continue working at the detail level in order to ensure ongoing progress. By removing yourself from the physical presence in the endless meetings, you ensure you will be forgotten as an individual and soon become just another faceless "resource". At this point, the less said and seen the better off you are. You will have given your team leaders the necessary information to bury any unpleasant results in the tangle of acronym-speak and documentation.

VM-Success

At the Inertial Determinate Point, just as the project is about to shift from stationary to "in motion", you will have the option of stepping deeper into the day-to-day project management by a policy of planting ever-increasing volumes of information for your project team. This information serves as the basis for defining project success at a future point. While others will take on the survival task of generating documentation – and the more the better –, you will continue to move forward with a high profile participation in as many meetings as you can manage to attend. At this stage, much like Hollywood actors, any publicity is good for your career. It is all about name recognition since your intent is to make yourself known as far up the chain of command as possible.

By becoming a vocal participant in the project, you gain the advantage of recognition and of influence. There is a distinguishing difference between being vocally active and actually active. The VM-Manager in success mode is trying to avoid work and substitutes talk for it. You will be in the prime position to influence the information delivered to management and be able to work on your own Department of

Intentional Failure strategy if needed. At this time, you must develop a multi-pronged strategy, naming everyone within striking distance as the proximal cause of failure. This will provide you with insurance both up and down the chain so you may select the most appropriate failure point should specific events require you to activate a failure.

Overcoming Inertia -Take That Mr. Newton!

Stopping the project can be even harder than getting it started. For one thing, it is always more fun to begin than to finish. As time passes, difficulties emerge, and fatigue begins to take its toll as change after change wears down the team, it is important to monitor those around you carefully. In either the survival or success positions, the activity around you will dictate whether the inertial effects are in your favor or are heading you toward the cliff.

As the old proverb states, time and tide wait for no man. Inertia, when applied to project management, means that getting underway is a bit like pushing your stalled car up a very steep driveway. You are going to need a lot of help and you want to know if pushing from the back is a good idea. What happens if it suddenly starts to roll backward and you are staring at the license plate as the rest of the team leaps to the side? Perhaps you would prefer to be alongside the vehicle, pressing against the open window frame. A leap to safety is a whole lot easier. On the other hand, once underway a project is a bit like an airplane that is merrily cruising along while flying over a beautiful mountain range. In this case, you had better have a plan in case the engine quits. Believe me, the guy flying the plane (in this case the project manager or sponsor) will have a parachute. What about you?

VM-PM - Develop Products More Quickly

A common difficulty faced by all of us is the need to complete things on time. Whether that is a plan to get your yard mowed before the next rainstorm or one to complete a complex six-hundred hour coding task, there always seem to be things dropped in the way of your well thought out plan. Invariably, that has a negative impact on your schedule. In a VM-Organization, that can be disastrous. Or not. It really depends on how you approach this problem.

111

If timelines are a recurring problem for you, perhaps all you need to do is perfect your skills at Schedule Enhancement.

If you consider all the topics we have discussed thus far, it will be clear to you that a major component of the VM-Lifestyle involves the collection and distribution of large amounts of largely useless and undecipherable information. In fact, a successful VM-Project-Manager not only expects this but also relies on it.

While it may not have been immediately apparent, there are two main advantages of this information overload. The first, which we have already discussed, is the ability to prearrange blame. The clever VM project manager will have several potential targets in mind to assume blame for any anticipated failure of the current project. Buried in all that documentation which is in turn buried in complex repositories and strung out across multiple approval lines are any number of traps just waiting to be set and sprung. In conjunction with this preventative and protective activity lies another benefit.

The VM objective is to provide a shallow, Green Water view of the project. At the same time, because all projects are complex, it is nearly impossible for any one person to have more than a passing knowledge of the various activities underway. A good VM-Manager will also make all projects appear to be significantly more complex than they actually are. This is by design for future failure protection. It also has the effect of making schedules as indecipherable as the rest of the collected documentation. This confusion delivers an advantage to the VM-Manager.

The use of schedule manipulation is so simple that we are surprised it took us so long to uncover this secret. Schedules contain a delivery date for both component parts and the finished product. Schedules are complicated by nature and are made incomprehensible by the VM-Manger. Schedules can be changed and the only one privy to this fact is the changer. In this case, that is the crafty VM-Manager. The schedule has become so complex that without extensive study, no one outside the VM-Manager can unravel the details. Therefore, it is unlikely that anyone will question the situation.

Sadly, this is how it works: Want your project to appear to finish sooner? Change the content of the tasks and declare victory at a lower component level. Better yet, deliver what you currently have and then begin talking about Phase 2 (or 3 or 4 or 56) as though that were always part of the plan. Besides you, nobody will be able to puzzle out what just happened. Toss a few acronyms that you have invented to summarize your early completion success, then stand by, and wait to be invited to the pizza party to celebrate your success.

Launching the Lifeboat

Dear Messrs. Frank and Willard,

My daily calendar is festooned with meeting after meeting, day after day. Each morning starts with a team scrum followed by a mid-day and end-of day status call. In between there are meetings with product planners, customer representatives and clients, team members and other teams not to mention with my boss. In an average week, I spend nearly 30 hours in meetings and have to spend my own time to catch up on email and my assignments.

People schedule meetings with me whether the slot is open or not or whether the meeting is relevant to me or not. I haven't had even ten minutes for lunch in over a month. Having three or even four meetings at the same time happens frequently. If I don't show up they reschedule. Sometimes my boss berates me for not attending. The meetings I do make rarely conclude with any decisions reached. As there are no agendas this is hardly surprising. I'm beginning to wonder if all these meetings are an effort at quality improvement, keeping us from doing any work and thereby reducing any errors we might make.

Is there anything I can do to save my sanity and get something to eat during the day?

Hungry in Houston
==========
Dear Mr. Houston,

Meetings are like buses, if you miss one there will be another coming along soon. Maybe it will be headed where you want, maybe not — just like most meetings. Certainly, you need to plan your attendance judiciously; but whether your criterion is subject matter, possible refreshments or is politically motivated, that is up to you.

You have to remember that most meetings require your attendance as an audience member rather than as a contributor.

However, from the Veneer Management point of view, it can be rewarding to be a willing participant, or a meeting enabler, if you will. By accurately gauging the ebb and flow of the meeting, you can inject a comment or a question at the proper moment to indicate you've been paying attention and have a useful idea or two. You might be viewed as a valuable ally to one or more of the meeting organizers. The last thing you want to happen is to volunteer for any task that comes up in these meetings – the next meeting to appear on your schedule will be your own.

When you get hungry, look at your calendar and suddenly remember an off-site meeting and take your leave. It would help if you had a great exit line but a swift and quiet escape is good enough.

Frank and Willard

VM-PM - The Power and Purpose of the "Meeting"

There are many different types of meetings that appear like unwanted weeds in the garden of our daily calendars. There are informational meetings called to promote an exchange between individuals or groups. There are planning meetings, organizational meetings, review meetings, preliminary, intermediate and final approval meetings. Individual behavior in these meetings is defined by a large poster found tacked to one wall in every meeting room by the HR Department. Each person is aware of the role they play, particularly how to prolong any discussion by a well-timed question while posing as a devil's advocate or a request for a re-summarization of the discussion.

Generally, the purpose of these meetings is to showcase the VM-Skills of the VM-Manager. Occasionally, the goal of a meeting is to reach a consensus on a specified topic. Participation in these meetings is arranged such that an apparent agreement is reached but is purposely vague so that each attendee walks away with a different concept of the decision reached.

The foremost economist of his time, John Kenneth Galbraith, took note of the useful nature of VM-Business Meetings in his analysis for his 1954 book, *The Great Crash 1929*. In writing about the actions of the government leaders as the stock market went into free-fall, he described what occurred in this way:

> Yet to suppose that President Hoover was engaged only in organizing further reassurance is to do him a serious injustice. He was also conducting one of the oldest, most important – and unhappily, one of the least understood – rites in American life. This is the rite of the meeting, which is called not to do business but to do no business. It is a rite which is still much practiced in our time. It is worth examining for a moment.
>
> Men meet together for many reasons in the course of business. They need to instruct or persuade each other. They must agree on a course of action. They find thinking in public more productive or less painful than thinking in private. But there are at least as many reasons for meetings to transact no business. Meetings are held because men seek companionship or, at a minimum, wish to escape the tedium of solitary duties. They yearn for the prestige which accrues to the man who presides over meetings, and this leads them to convoke assemblages over which they can preside. Finally, there is the meeting, which is called not because there is business to be done, but because it is necessary to create the impression that business is being done. Such meetings are more than a substitute for action. They are widely regarded as action.
>
> The fact that no business is transacted at a no-business meeting is normally not a serious cause of embarrassment to those attending. Numerous formulas have been devised to prevent discomfort. Thus Scholars, who are great devotees of the no-business meeting, rely heavily on the exchange-of-ideas justification. To them the exchange of ideas is an absolute good. Any meeting at which ideas are exchanged is, therefore, useful. This justification is nearly ironclad. It is very hard to have a meeting of which it can be said that no ideas were exchanged.

VM-Managers have continued to refine the no-business meeting practice to a high art. When combined with a quest for consensus it becomes a useful work avoidance tool.

Launching the Lifeboat

Dear Mr. Frank and Mr. Willard,

The sales, product delivery and implementation cycle at my company moves at a glacial pace. I asked my management team to find changes that would fix this by simplifying the process and that could be implemented ASAP. After two months' time they returned with a hundred and fifty page PowerPoint presentation that took four hours and eight people to explain. Could I possibly have mis-communicated what I wanted?

Yours,
A. Bothered Executive
==========
Dear Abe,

Sometime when you ask for "sense" and you get "nonsense", you think maybe you should have asked for "nonsense". What you have experienced is the result of uncontrolled VM expressed in two forms: 1) consultants who are by their very function disassociated from your processes and 2) managers with axes to grind and domains to protect. Maybe you share some blame in setting a boundary-less task as it obviously became too big for them to handle. You must learn the rules to governing the process improvement kingdom in order to produce the result you want. Consult our revelations on this topic as soon as you can.

With Sympathy,
Frank-Willard

VM - Six Sigma and Process Improvements

The recognized methodology today to improve business processes includes Six Sigma, black belts and lean workouts. Just as a broken clock tells the right time twice a day, efforts to identify process improvements will occasionally produce useful results. This is clearly dependent upon the persons involved, their grasp of the subject matter, the strength of their pre-conceived notions and their honest intentions. Certainly, those who attend for a week of free lunches are not all that helpful. Nor are those who are focused on blocking any work shifted in their direction or who actively redirect work to someone else. After these sessions, the persons most satisfied with the results are usually those who began with a solution in mind and influenced the acceptance of it on the group.

In the past, businesses turned to "efficiency experts" to recommend ways to improve productivity and ultimately increase profits. These were commonly people well-schooled in all aspects of the business or the industry in question. After a thorough review, they were able to point out changes to put the business on track.

Current practice employs facilitators who act more like psychologists asking what changes feel right or acupuncturists looking for pain points. Facilitators guide the group, not to arrive at the best solutions but to exercise the techniques they have been taught, like the 5 Whys and the Pareto Chart. To establish their bona fides they talk about having learned Japanese in order to help Toyota trim ten minutes off their production line. They keep the process moving forward conducting brain storming sessions under a swirling Cosmic Stupidity Cloud. Lots of ideas are expected from these sessions, which are marked, by no criticism and no instant analysis and where no ideas are rejected. The facilitators marshal the group from activity to activity like some frenzied party organizer. When everyone stops to take a breath the conference rooms are papered with colored post-it notes, looking like a piñata exploded.

The fun starts when each attendee is asked to vote for the top three to five ideas to explore in depth. Voting in the lean workout is much like electing the prom King and Queen. Some politicking goes on and popularity has an effect on the voting. Through careful observation, the VM-Manager can cast strategic votes to influence the final tally increasing the chances that the choices will have little impact on his department or team. The most successful workouts occur when the ideas are spread across a variety of groups, the least when every idea targets the same team.

After the votes are counted, small cross-functional task groups are formed to investigate and detail the winning ideas. The VM-Manager's role is to be a positive and willing participant, presenting an attitude of openness to change, however the real strategy is to shift focus to other groups and departments where rich opportunities for improvements exist. When faced with alterations to his area, the VM-Manager will employ stalling tactics and press for more investigation and detail rather than show any opposition. The goal is to avoid accepting any material change or make such changes dependent on those in another area.

The results of the workouts are communicated to the sponsors by daily report outs. This assures the sponsors that the effort will produce something useful. These are given by spokespersons for the sub-groups tasked with detailing one or more of the selected improvement ideas under the eye of the facilitator, beaming with pride like a schoolteacher watching prize pupils recite their lines. Any manager, the VM-Manager included, will arrange to avoid giving a presentation. This is to preserve the impression that "management" had no influence over the recommendations. If asked to do so, it is best that the subject is related to some other manager's responsibilities.

On the last day of the workout, the final report out is given. The solidified proposals are presented with specific attention paid to next steps. This is commonly when the attempt to improve processes breaks down. Frequently the suggestions contain some innate level of impracticality. The potential benefit is stressed but the suggestions require wholesale revisions to processes, reorganization of multiple departments or lots more staff in order to implement them. The details are intentionally glossed over. The facilitator and the sponsor declare success and everyone returns to their day jobs.

The obvious conclusion is that if you really want to know how to improve things then ask the people who do the work about practical suggestions they can make – oh, that's right, they were let go in the last reduction in force.

VM - Risk Assessment and Quality Assurance

Risk Assessment and Quality Assurance are key components in all product development. It is critically important to protect one's customers as well as the business from potential harm through both physical and fiscal danger. Reference was made earlier to product improvements that have benefited the consumer while enhancing the prestige of the manufacturer. Safety and Quality are two touchstones which never fail to catch your attention. No one will ever argue against those items any more than they would argue against the importance of Mom and apple pie.

Risk Assessment

It has been necessary to create administrative bodies to ensure that the manufacturers as well as the consumers create and use products in a responsible manner. To support their charter, voluminous documents regulating corporate and personal behavior while also protecting the work force and the environment have been published. There is a natural antagonism between these segments, which further complicates matters. In the effort to get it right, thousands of hours and millions of dollars are spent producing hundreds of thousands of pages of analysis and regulations. The "deep dive" is a particularly valuable tool in this endeavor although it can be moderated by the political importance of the issue under study. The amount of time spent prior to crafting new legislation or regulations is frequently abbreviated depending on the financial, political or emotional nature of the issue linked to a highly charged public demand for action.

Who is tasked with making the assessments and determining what regulations may then apply varies according to the size of the enterprise. Small businesses will assign such work on an ad hoc basis as the needs arise. Larger ones will have whole departments dedicated to ferreting out both risks and those who may generate them. Such departments may be found on the organizational hierarchy chart as independent bodies or subordinate to the legal departments. There is often a suspicion that they either belong to or are an alias for the Department of Intentional Failure.

Both regulation writers and risk assessors walk a fine line between over-regulation or over-alerting and serving the industry or business instead of satisfying their charter to ensure safety and quality. Imposing stringent rules or the wrong rules can have unintended consequences, eliminating useful products or making a bad situation worse. Evaluating too many events as high risk or passing the risk condition with minimal attention can be just as detrimental, reducing the impact of an evaluation or creating an impression of white-washing the issues. There must be a balance between good intentions, however misguided and seemingly aimless, and the obsessive application of the printed regulations.

The intersection of VM and Risk Assessment can be either a chance for the VM-Manager to shine or to be cast back into the shadows. The latter can occur when the VM-Manager has failed to generate the raw material needed to satisfy risk assessments. Project schedules are impacted when staff is reallocated to do the assessments and as a punishment for the lack of preparation the most stringent criteria is applied with no exceptions allowed. There is no glory to be found in this effort as it will be predominately a paper-work task and rarely, if ever, revealing actual risks. Unrecoverable failure will occur for the VM-Manager who overlooks this very real project hazard.

The multiplicity of documents and acronyms offers the VM-Manager opportunities to produce reams of paper. The VM-Manager can be proactive by establishing a Risk Condition Minimalization Program (RCMP) by which the least amount of effort can be expended in producing the most amount of supporting documentation as to why there are no risks or how any risks that exist have been dealt with in the project. Delaying a project due to unacceptable risks is a legitimate option and reflects well on the whistle blower. However, by careful pre-planning the VM-Manager can avoid this step by having prepared an Amalgamated Action Retirement Policy (AARP) indicating how the next project (and the next VM-Manager) will correct any flaws.

Quality Assurance

Quality, like the old saw about beauty, is in the eye of the beholder. That is, quality has a variable definition based on the person making that determination, their role in the organization and the discipline to which they belong.

Grand religious debates can occur over how to determine quality. Executives want to know if the standard practices were followed. Risk management wants to know if all the forms were filled out, any corrective steps documented and all labeling is in place. Implementation management wants to know if all the documentation is up to date. Documentation management wants to know if the documents are accessible and the spelling and grammar are correct. The shipping department wants to know if the manifest is complete. Test management wants to know if all the tests were run and the results documented. Design and development management wants to know if all the right meetings were held, the feedback documented, the artifacts created and that each person finished their assignments on time. Determining that things actually work is apparently a byproduct of individual tasks.

There are two basic pillars to quality assurance: standards and documentation. Each discipline has its own standards to apply and artifacts to document that those standards were upheld. In VM, the dominant quality measure is process standards. If the VM-Manager can answer the question as to whether all processing steps were followed with "Yes," then it is assumed that the completed project meets quality standards.

Certainly all the disciplines employed on a project must also live up to their own standards and demonstrate that they do so. What the VM-Manager is alert to is a change to any of those standards which threaten the project if applied after the fact. To maintain the "just enough" effort criteria, the VM-Manager will resist this potential drain on the project to change something that did not matter yesterday and will likely not matter tomorrow. A concept that assists the VM-Manager in this goal is Retroactive Validation – also known as the "Grandfather Clause". This is customarily invoked to avoid the implementation of standards retroactively.

There is a variant usage of Retroactive Validation when applied to testing. Essentially this is used as a justification for not executing or developing a test suite. The basic rationale is, "It worked before; we didn't change it so it must work now."

The need to pass the quality hurdle encourages the VM-Manager to shun the Quick and Dirty Methodology (QaDM). As QaDM rarely produces the necessary supporting artifacts, following that method will not afford the VM-Manager the opportunity to manufacture progress through documentation. As QaDM dies out, the VM-Managers and the products they develop will naturally benefit from quality standards.

VM - Validation and Verification

The VM-Manager's project must meet the stated needs and utility of that project as interpreted in the validation phase and rendered in an appropriate manner as interpreted in the verification phase. Assuming that the needs (requirements) were identified, that the design steps addressed those needs, and that all steps in planning, organization and production or execution followed the set of mandated processes, each step confirmed by documented approvals garnered at the conclusion of each phase, the outcome can only be successful. Consequently, the necessity for validation and verification becomes a mere formality to be accomplished with a minimum expenditure of time and effort.

Validation Phase

Where the project requirements have been written in the prescribed VM manner, the wording will be such that any result can be interpreted as satisfying the original need. The VM-Manager must prepare for the validation review to deploy any obfuscation strategy to re-interpret the needs in correspondence with the actual outcome or to alter the scope to exclude any outliers from the plan. The goal is to declare success and move on.

Verification Phase

In keeping with the core concept of minimalization in VM-Management, the verification phase is focused on the current product version and current set of alterations and additions. Examination of features or functions beyond the immediate area is deemed outside the scope of the present effort. To expand the scope would seriously affect the time-lines and require additional staff to accomplish as well as additional staff to deal with the results. A principle the VM-Manager will always observe is, "Do not test anything you do not intend to fix!"

Objective evidence is required of the status and number of tests performed. The purpose is not to indicate any sense of effort required or the effectiveness of the process. For instance, there is no need to record how many failures were identified over time or how many executions of any one test script was required before it was marked complete. Nor is there any quantification of scripts included versus function points covered or required to be covered. Previously long hours would be spent in defining who, what, where, and when for this phase. In VM-Methodology, regardless of the actual effort required, everything is marked complete with no failures, and success is declared. Any unavoidable issues become an opportunity for the next program once they are correctly explained and deferred.

It must be recalled that "quality" has a variable definition according to one's role. By attesting that all steps followed the prescribed processes, the VM-Manager ensures a positive quality evaluation. However, there is sometimes a dissenting opinion arising outside the corporate environment from external sources such as the user community. This often confuses the upper echelon of management who firmly hold to the certainty that quality is an assumed state which occurs automatically by following established processes – quality becomes a "given". Nevertheless, this does not deter upper management from asking why certain flaws were not found in the verification phase. There is often a fantastical assumption that verification not only examined the current changes but that all previously existing functionality was covered through regression steps. While rarely voiced, the common reaction by the VM-Manager is on the order of "60,000 function points, they can't all work – and don't even think about testing them!"

The Mythos of Testing - Using CHIMERA

All development plans include one or more test cycles. The content of each cycle is frequently a topic for debate where the arguments vary according to the individuals' point of view. The test plan becomes a catch-all in an attempt to cover why it is being done (purpose), who is doing it (responsibility), what the extent is (scope, when it is done (timing, where it is being done (environment), how it is done (methodology), and lastly, is it proven (auditability). The cost to meet the expectations of these factors can be significant in both time and dollars.

The VM-Manager will grapple with these concepts and determine how they affect his or her project. Then through minimalization, will apply thin, lean and mean strategies to manage time lines and resource allocations.

Rather than address the question of what to test, the VM-Manager seeks to determine if testing is a necessary part of the program or if it is a luxury that can be trimmed to meet budgetary needs and project schedules. Building on the sentiment, "You can't test in quality" VM shifts the focus of testing to the development organization. The VM-Manager may argue that testing outside the needs of basic development is an unproductive and valueless expense. Certainly this assertion gains traction where the number of flaws reported by the user community and the engineering staff, regularly exceed the number reported by the verification team.

If the development staff can shoulder more of the testing load, can the test team be cut back? Following this path the VM-Manager can not only affect the project schedule he will gain credibility as a cost-cutter as "excess" positions are trimmed.

Why should we test? The answer to this seems self-evident. Certainly products must be validated. Doing so is almost a pure behavioral exercise, which includes a component designed to determine limits and to measure performance. There is also a functional validation component to demonstrate that all the requirements have been met. VM meets the challenge through its customary minimalization approach. The focus of each test cycle is isolated to the modifications and additions applied in this current increment. Having shifted the onus of testing to the development team, the test team is virtually freed of creating its own test scenarios and draws on those already written and exercised by the developers.

A risk the VM-Manager must account for is action taken by the Department of Intentional Failure against either phase. For example, the validation phase may be delayed by introducing a new means of recording, encoding and collating user needs. The verification phase can be derailed by requiring new tools, new recording methods and new statistical measurements or simply a change in reporting format.

To address possible external criticism as to the lack of quality, seven generalized verification methods have been identified and assigned the mnemonic CHIMERA:

C heck List – Three functions required – three functions executed
H istorical – (1+2=3) from today = (1+2=3) from last execution
I dentity – (1+2=3) identical to (2+1=3)
M athematical – (1+2=3) verified by reversal (3-2=1)
E xistence – a$\int$x where row 'a' is created with 10 fields all with content
R elationship – a$\int$y where for each a, 2 b's are created (A:B as 1:2); thus given 10 a's there should be 20 b's
A pproximation – a$\int$z where for each a 1 to 2 b's are created; thus given 10 a's there should be between 10 and 20 b's; 15 is reasonable, 25 is out of range

Through the consistent application of these techniques, the VM-Manager is assured of a product that has reached a modicum of testing beyond that of a fantasy.

VM - Life Cycle

To this point, we have covered the impact of VM on the developmental aspects of a project. The transitional steps from development to an installation, implementation and production stage would be the natural next steps to cover. The authors prefer to exercise the VM-Approach and declare that at this time, those topics are out of scope. Look for the next edition of this book to include them. Instead, we will jump to the maintenance aspects as this becomes a fruitful topic for discussion.

Throughout the development phase, we have noted the technique of redefining content to fit an arbitrary schedule with tasks that have actually been completed. Each successive phase or increment is saddled with the sins of omission committed by the previous increment - tasks that did not make the cut. This produces the familiar "known defects" list. This generally continues until it becomes necessary to establish an actual "done" state. Fortunately for the VM-Manager (Development) the definition of "done" is variable. Unfortunately for the VM-Manager (Installation) this tends to create an unreasonable expectation of completeness.

At the end of most projects, a maintenance phase is immediately begun, driven by the number and importance of the leftover tasks. Often the product just released will not function or will be labeled immediately as NFFP (Not Fit For Purpose). This is not necessarily broadcast widely leaving the VM-Manager (Installation) in the dark, blissfully establishing his own project schedule unaware of the need to handle subsequent releases. The naïve VM-Manager will express shock to find that the product she was just handed does not actually work even though it was declared "done" by the development agency.

After this bumpy period passes, all the maintenance releases, service packages and hot fixes have been delivered, the maintenance phase shifts to client reported issues. This is not to say that all the other leftover work has been completed. It is now mixed in with issues reported from outside the company. This creates a divisive dynamic between the former project team and the support staff over the matter of priorities. The solution is often to throw all the items into the same pot and have a committee review each one and establish a relative priority. It is not always necessary that the members of the committee have an intimate knowledge of the issue or the product. It is enough that they are familiar with the client reporting the issue or that they have some control over resource allocation and timelines. This is an event of some importance to VM-Managers as it offers a ripe opportunity to shift work to others within the organization.

Under this process, the backlog of issues becomes greater and greater until its very size becomes an issue. The VM-Manager (Support) has several options but must first exhibit a form of due diligence. This is done by exercising the "Maximization of Minimalization" principle in assigning one or more persons outside the committee to evaluate the entire backlog. Contrary to the "just enough" approach the VM-Manager would apply to himself, here he asks that a considerable effort be expended to produce what will be a minimal amount of information, in effect, invoking the deep dive spell. That is, any decision made with respect to the backlog will not be based on prioritization identified by this effort. Rather, it will be based more in terms of influence and expediency. The common solution is to simply close the oldest items and remove them from any further status report.

Should any of these items be classified with a high priority or criticality, the committee will review them and lower the priority to permit their closure.

This becomes an annual event with some projects. The dramatic alteration in the statistics on outstanding issues frequently provides a springboard for the VM-Manager (Support) to move up in the management hierarchy. Many top-level executives found the fast track in this way.

Eventually management will sunset a product. In all likelihood, the final VM-Manager for this project will see the sun go down on their career as well, so it is important to be aware of this ever-present risk. It may come through simple obsolescence, replacement by new development or the sudden acquisition of a competing product. The VM-Manager in this position must have already prepared the ground for the next move on the hierarchy chart. This involves making his role unnecessary for the current project by delegating all responsibility to his subordinates. At the same time, he is making himself indispensable through the techniques and tactics noted later in "Managing Up the Hierarchy". As the project floats off to a Viking funeral, the VM-Manager steps ashore with his broadsword at the ready.

Summary

The Project Management discipline has become an integral part of all businesses and is intended to ensure the proper controls are applied and the proper results are obtained for projects. However, as we all know the possession of a certificate does not equate to skill. Further, the passing of a test may measure short-term memory (rather than real knowledge) but certainly not an ability to use it. VM has found this to be a fertile environment to grow and prosper.

Goal setting is important in defining the purpose and scope of any project. A well-crafted plan can provide a way to keep a project from unwanted additions as well as from wandering from the path. The key is to outline business aims over product aims. A dash of ambiguity allows an amount of wiggle-room in which the VM-Manager can operate.

Good planning will ensure the survival of the VM-Manager regardless of the success or failure of the project at hand. Creating a massive complex of interrelated documents that requires the technical writing equivalent of a forensic accountant to unravel will make this happen. It is said in war and politics that the map is not the territory – in VM the like sentiment is that the plan is not the project but sometimes the plan is the product, especially as a model for the next project.

VM-Projects are always successful. Certainly, they can end in different ways but the common features are that they do end and usually disappear without any ripples on the corporate pond. These projects may complete by actually reaching the end of the plan or may be declared to be complete followed by a brief clean-up phase. Most often, the state at the present moment is declared as the definition of both complete and success and the team reassigned to the next project.

All projects are subject to operational inertia. They are often tough to get moving and may even be harder to stop. Having overcome inertia at the beginning, the VM-Manager observes project trends to identify the Inertial Determinate Point (IDP). At that instant, a crucial decision is required from the VM-Manager which will determine his continued survival or success within the organization.

VM-Scheduling serves two purposes: 1) promote the apparent complexity while demonstrating progress against the timeline; and 2) provide opportunities for rapid revamping of the timeline for a shorter path to success.

Meetings are a key component of VM. A project plan filled with multiple recurring meetings gives an immediate impression of control and activity. The fact that little or nothing is accomplished is a long-standing tradition in American business, right after the three-martini lunch.

The drive for process improvements through Six Sigma and lean workouts is open to manipulation. This is done through pre-selecting apathetic participants or ones with preconceived notions. The VM-Manager has an offensive and defensive role to play in these sessions according to the agenda that best serves their project and ambitions.

128

Risk Assessment and Quality Assurance represent two areas where a project can be derailed through the best of intentions. The VM-Manager can resist these forces or embrace them depending upon his own goals. The best approach is to find a way to make standards work for you.

VM-Managers have vivid imaginations and are able to draw outsiders into their vision of the world as they describe exciting possibilities through compelling visual constructs and verbal gymnastics. A story with flash rather than substance with a perception of value just within reach will make it all believable.

Testing, like documentation, frequently falls victim to schedule changes and budget cuts. Test plans are constructed with this in mind concentrating on the minimum set of tests to execute. The validation and verification teams should not look left or right but stay focused on completing just enough tests to complete the cycle. If you must test, be certain to follow a supportable method such as CHIMERA.

The opportunities for a VM-Manager continue as a project enters the normal post-development life cycle. The maintenance and support arena allows the full exercise of techniques of schedule and content manipulation to be coupled with manufactured statistics showing trends to support any argument the VM-Manager cares to make. As a product reaches its sunset years, the VM-Manager will already be positioned to move to the next step on the Corporate Escalator.

MANAGING THE DIALOGUE

Launching the Lifeboat

Dear Mr. Frank and Mr. Willard

After spending nearly ten years of my life in this business, I've started to wonder if I have a brain tumor. I sit in meeting after meeting listening to other team members discuss topics which I thought I understood only to come away more confused. Lately I have noticed that everyone, including the managers, seems comfortable with the conversation – everyone, that is, but me.

I used to stop the discussion and ask for a translation of what had just been said. It wasn't long before I noticed the smirks and heard mumbled comments when I interrupted this way. I was clueless when the team started referring to crawlback strategies, pivot positions, de-duplication and OMG, re-de-duplication!

Am I missing something here? Am I in the wrong business or should I schedule a CAT scan?

Anxious Alice, Austin, TX
==========
Dear Alice.

You can cancel your appointment in radiology. There is nothing wrong with your brain and you have not passed through the looking glass - though you may have fallen down a rabbit hole. Your reaction marks you as the sanest and most intelligent member of the team. At least you had the sense to ask, "What the hell is going on?"

Biologists have identified plants and animals as indicator species. Canaries are used in coal mines because through their sensitivity to environmental change they will exhibit the first symptoms of a situation gone wrong. In the same way, people can sense the onset of VM as language changes. The introduction of made up words, meaningless acronyms and the constant use of both in communications signal the growing presence of VM in your company.

The source of your anxiety is a subconscious recognition that these words and acronyms are simply gibberish, injected in the conversation to heighten the "perception" of competence. You alert these lexicographers that you are on to their charade by asking for definitions. They react by dismissing your concerns. It is pure defensive posturing on their part.

You have a choice to make. You can sit on the sidelines ignoring the hogwash, or you can join in the game and create your own dictionary of meaningless words. Feel free to toss them into any discussion. No one will question you as that will expose them as not being on board the VM movement.

Our advice to you is to study the section on "Managing the Dialogue" and apply the lessons learned. It is not about what you say; it's about how you say it. Don't forget: "All mimsy were the borogoves and the mome raths outgrabe."

Frank and Willard

VM-Manager - A Central Role

It is an old cliché that information is power. As a conduit between upper management and staff, the VM-Manager is in a position to control the flow of information in both directions. These managers act as a filter in the upward direction passing items that are positive and for which they can claim credit. In the downward direction, these managers color the items by assuming an air of superior knowledge and privileged access thus taking on and wearing the authority of upper management.

This works exceedingly well in those organizations where senior managers want little contact with the staff and vice versa. A VM-Manager with the right mix of ambition and guile can insert himself into the power structure with a little imagination and almost no effort.

The only threat, of course, is the "skip-level" interview where these two normally uncommunicative bodies might interact. Having little routine contact with each other, the information exchanged is almost certainly to be misunderstood by both parties. By working to manage the dialog in both directions, the VM-Manager can handle even this situation.

Managing Up or Managing Down - What's Your Flavor?

The answer to this question really depends on whether the VM-Manager has career aspirations or intends to maintain the status quo by staying in the present position. The nature of the information in either direction is the same: no one wants to hear bad news; no one wants to be criticized; everyone wants to feel free to complain. It is the VM-Manager's job to fulfill these needs in both directions. The basic interaction from lower to upper is always the same. If you are going to tell me about a problem, you had better also tell me how you solved it.

Managing Up the Hierarchy

Try as you might, it is almost impossible to practice upward delegation. However, the pretense of doing so can only work with less-experienced peers who are not yet VM-Managers. By indicating you are referring to or consulting with a superior, one advertises a relationship that excludes the other managers. Having assumed a level of prestige not afforded to other managers, you can sometimes advance a ploy of inducing them to pass information through your auspices or even performing work for you, further enhancing your position in the management hierarchy while easing your workload.

Another means of "managing up" is through the control of information by the VM-Manager using LIFT tools - Less Information Faster Technology. These tools embody the principle of providing less information faster for ease of consumption. They are used in most every organization today. The customary vehicle is a single PowerPoint slide in a standardized format. In larger organizations, this allows for the weekly status reports across multiple programs and projects to follow the same presentation and accelerates the review. The formats vary slightly but the content is the same, distilled to the bare minimum. Items covered include the near-term portion of the project timeline, current task and status, potential risks and their color rating, and a graph or pie chart indicating the progress against the plan. Calculating progress in terms of burn down numbers inserts a visually dynamic sense of progress. Issues and trends are highlighted by the use of color-coding to simplify executive interpretation.

The seasoned VM-Manager is aware of the suspicion thrown on a project that is always in the green zone, that is, one that never experiences troubles. Conversely, that manager also knows that showing serious trouble with one or more items in the red or danger zone reflects badly on their ability to manage a project. It is better to have occasional yellow highlighted items and accompany them with the description of how they were identified, caught before turning red and are moving back to a controlled green state. The reappearance of green status for this item at the next status meeting serves to demonstrate the exceptional competence of the VM-manager. These status meetings are not forums for presenting problems and asking for assistance or direction. If you have not already solved the problem, for heaven's sake do not bring it up.

The VM-Manager is constantly alert to the potential weaknesses of his peers in these review sessions. There may be an implication in a presentation not noticed by the senior staff that suggests a hidden risk to some other manager's project. Or there may have been some information gleaned outside the meeting that was conveniently omitted during the review. Using this information, the VM-Manager can claim a certain level of acumen in asking what appears to be an innocuous question that puts someone else on the spot. In this manner, she casually assumes a role as a senior manager and others will begin to see her as such. The gambit works well if exercised before she is called upon to review her own project as it can divert attention away from any weaknesses in her presentation and may even derail the session altogether.

There are times when the VM-Manager must approach senior managers with a proposal for a new project or possibly a change to an existing project. The common method of getting a sales pitch across is the "elevator speech", a five minute or less rapid-fire summary of what it is you want, why you need it, what it will do, what it will cost and why the senior manager should agree to it. The rationale behind this is not that most senior managers are afflicted by Attention Deficit Disorder or that they have administrative assistants that guard their calendars and office doors like a Gorgon. Rather, it is believed to be the most direct means of getting across all those previous points in the shortest possible amount of time. To do so you must focus on the most significant aspects, particularly low cost, least effort and most positive effect on the senior manager's career advancement.

Managing Down the Hierarchy

Most organizations make a distinction between the human resources manager and the functional manager. On the surface, this separation allows the former to focus on the busy-work of a manager: performance reports, training plans, and vacation scheduling while the latter focuses on the actual day-to-day work. When the persons in these roles work well together, it can be a very successful dynamic, especially when the functional manager has a strong background in the work. In practice, the human resource role is generally shifted to the functional manager and the HR duties soon become the dominant focus for the manager. As this human resource activity begins absorbing more and more time, the functional manager's technical role decreases and can ultimately disappear.

Knowing this, the VM-Manager must camouflage their domain to minimize the effect of any technical shortcomings caused by their decreasing involvement. The most common method is to put pressure on the staff through the imposition of short time lines. The human resources role then comes to the forefront. Random elements such as completing training assignments, attending mandatory meetings, writing performance reviews for the current year and planning for the next year can take time away from the work schedule. Blame for the inability to complete a task or to perform in a technically competent manner can be shifted to the team member.

Much like a lawyer in a courtroom, the VM-Manager never asks a question in a staff meeting for which he does not already have the answer. These meetings, like the project review meetings, are not for identifying problems or resolving them. The VM-Manager's approach is "Don't court trouble, don't tolerate trouble." The main purpose of these meetings is to ensure that everyone on the team has more than one assignment; that they are in fact overloaded so that there is no chance of any of them telling a senior manager that they have nothing to do.

The VM-Manager routinely transmits messages from senior management to the staff. When the message is positive, the VM-Manager can easily tailor the delivery to garner credit for it by suggesting some influence in making it happen. When the message is negative, the VM-Manager can still gain sympathy from his team by expressing his personal opposition that was, unfortunately, overruled by business needs.

There are occasions when upper management requires a communication blanket to be spread over the organization. This is like the quiet period before an IPO is issued. It is called for when the economic position of the business is in turmoil and significant changes are in the works, particularly reductions in staff. VM-Managers are asked to use their skills at manipulating perceptions down the hierarchy, manufacturing positive messages to the work force. In these situations it is important for the VM-Manager to curb any speculations while encouraging the employees to "stay the course" until they are no longer useful. Sometimes it is difficult for the VM-Manager to feign interest in this process such as the one who felt compelled to say, "If you haven't quit by now, you need to stay on board."

Inventing Your Own Vocabulary

English is the dominant language for exchanging information wherever a U.S. business is involved. It has its limitations based on common usage as well as the knowledge and experience levels of both the speaker and the listener. Miscommunication, especially when gathering requirements, is always present. Everyone is familiar with the simple problem presented by weather versus whether or present (now) versus present (gift) or the more complicated rain, rein, reign. Many businesses, but software houses in particular, are notorious for using the same word to mean widely different things where even the context does not provide a clue to the meaning.

Though English is an imperfect tool it is the one being used, and like democracy, we Americans believe it is superior to all other options. English is a dynamic, acquisitive language. It is extensible through adopting words from virtually all other languages as opposed to German where new words are constructed by appending other words until the result looks and reads like a sentence written by William Faulkner.

English can be further modified by usage where words previously identified as nouns are repurposed as verbs. These words can take on new meanings seemingly at odds with the original. This capability lends itself to the VM-Manager by allowing for the creation of a new vocabulary within the scope of one project, which, through careful application, can obscure that project and begin to affect others. Voicing the new vocabulary in an assured manner in the right settings will elevate the prestige of the VM-Manager as the inventor of new concepts and one who is at the leading edge of management techniques and processes. When these terms are echoed back in other settings by different persons, the VM-Manager will sense his or her effect on the organization as a whole.

Each discipline or product or business already has a base vocabulary that lends itself to ready manipulation by the VM-Manager. Examples are easy to identify and are usually accompanied by the immediate thought, "That's not a real word, is it?" One need not be bound by such considerations and the utility of these words will be proven by their acceptance and persistent usage. Words like "technologize" and "productize" have been in the lexicon for years. Attaching a suffix like "ist", "ite", "ize" to any word commonly used in your business will get you started.

Other suggestions are to borrow words from businesses, industries, or scientific disciplines separate from your own and adapt the more colorful ones for your own purposes. Particularly valuable are those businesses and products which enjoy popularity at the moment. Borrowing from the language that describes them will associate you with their success. Use these words often enough and with enough self-assurance and they will begin to survive on their own. You will establish lines of communication regardless of any meaningful content or context that exists because you have determined that it does exist. An example of this approach follows.

The Application of Grayscale in Communication

The VM-Manager must become adept at Grayscale Communication. In the visual spectrum, grayscale is a range of shades of gray without apparent color. The darkest possible shade is black while the lightest possible shade is white. In the communication spectrum, it is not a simple yin and yang of factual and non-factual, known and unknown, or complete and incomplete. Rather it is a measure of signal to noise ratio where the noise is indistinguishable from the signal and may actually be the signal. It is the VM-Manager's goal to remain firmly between these two poles where all communication takes on an ambiguity that nonetheless promotes the recognition of the VM-Manager as a subject matter expert, the infamous and sought after SME.

Shades of Gray - 1

Terminology, not technology is a key strength of the VM-Manager. Even so, knowing the definitions of the terms is not as important as simply knowing the right time to trot them out in a meeting. The verbal skills of the VM-Manager are less focused on conveying actual or even factual information than on firmly establishing that he or she knows more about the topic than the listener does. The successful VM-Manager will memorize the language patterns appropriate to his or her area of responsibility much like learning the dialogue for Spanish class. *The signal here is: I know something you do not.*

Shades of Gray - 2

The concept applies to written communications as well as verbal. The nature of any written communication can both reveal and promote the significance of the author. There is an inverse relationship between the importance of the author and their written communications in terms of word count: the fewer words used, the more important the author must be within the organization. By employing fewer words the purpose of the message becomes a reminder to the recipient that the sender is involved and is paying attention. The successful VM-Manager will use this knowledge when communicating with staff and peers, being certain to include a common signature block – "Sent from my Blackberry" or "Sent from my iPad". A brief, cryptic message obviously sent on the run, re-enforces the significance of the VM-Manager to the recipients.

The signal here is three-fold: I am important and busy but took a moment to tell you so.

Shades of Gray - 3

The VM-Manager can utilize this technique in channels outside the nominal reporting hierarchy. By broadcasting minimalist congratulatory messages acknowledging other team's successes, the VM-Manager can enhance his corporate reputation. Though never directly or even indirectly associated with the event, these messages can influence the opinions up the management chain by maintaining the visibility of the VM-Manager while associating his or her name with a success.
The signal here is: Remember me; I know a good thing when I see it.

Down the chain the messages suggest that such approval of the result is significant, something to be sought.
The signal here is: My recognition of your success is important because I am important to know.

Shades of Gray - 4

A more daring use of this technique can be employed when presented with the announcement of failures. Here the VM-Manager can draw on terminology, the more arcane the better, to indicate that some foreknowledge of the situation existed to which they were privy. The risk here is that the VM-Manager might be seen as piling on or as an agent for the Department of Intentional Failure, or worst case, the failure may be a temporary setback and the situation rescued by a competing manager and team. The artful VM-Manager will have accounted for this latter possibility and prepared a follow-up congratulation message that accounts for the earlier criticism or even more boldly ignore that it had even occurred.
The signal here is: I would have made the right decision in the first place.

Shades of Gray – A Popular Approach

Certainly, the VM-Manager will encounter other VM-Managers employing these same techniques. It must be remembered that the audience for these communications are less your peers than their staff, your staff and both of your bosses. The recommendation here is to be vigilant, seizing every opportunity to be first with your messages and to keep your name at the forefront of every success. Note that you do not actually have to be a VM-Manager to employ these techniques. Any staff member can adopt this mode of communication and assume the mantle of the VM-Manager and his attendant successes. Encouraging selected members of your staff to follow these precepts will tend to divert the attention of other VM-Managers allowing you to interact more freely with your bosses.

Grayscale Information Exchange (GIE)

A variant usage of the Grayscale concept appears in other areas which can be loosely described as "information exchange". The metaphor here is taken from print processes where output can be produced using grayscale rather than high density, full color-quality output in order to save on ink. Grayscale Information Exchange describes the degradation that occurs due to indiscriminate replication with little or no attention given to maintaining identity.

The manufacturing industry depends on the production of "units" that are identical in every measurable way. When a unit fails to meet tolerances, it is discarded. The use of mechanical devices and computerized processes insure this level of quality control. The introduction of the human element in information exchange produces a different outcome.

GIE is a result of employing variable techniques to replicate an entity. The purpose is to produce a "copy" or "clone" of the original in a useable form or state. Humans, through their expression of individuality and independence, or pure cussedness, will not use the same techniques or follow the same steps with each replication. The danger in GIE is that the recipient makes an unfounded assumption that the entity received is identical in every way to the original. There is a superficial resemblance but the end product is different in subtle ways.

The situation is made worse by repeating the replication over and over, not from the original but from each succeeding copy. This is like the children's game of Telephone where a message is whispered in the ear of the first child who whispers it to the next and the next until it reaches the last one in line. The final message bears little resemblance to its original content.

Mechanical language translators exhibit a similar behavior often producing the oddest results from what seem the simplest inputs. One example of an English to Russian to English translation resulted in this axiom "The spirit is willing but the body is weak," reproduced as "The vodka is strong but the meat is rotten." The sense of the message is there but is barely understandable.

The impact in the VM-World is commonly seen within development environments. Imperfect replication mechanisms are employed which result in a grayscale information exchange. Quality and performance become degraded through constant replication. The VM-Manager must be on guard to detect when outside agencies affect his or her program in such a manner. "My system is a grayscale copy of the original" is a signal of a pending failure.

Whether speaking of a development environment, language translators, or telephone messages, our intention is to convey the notion that the item in hand may be an imitation of the parent version. The intrinsic value is not the same as the original, much as a photocopy of a dollar is not valued at a dollar. Further, the utility of the item is not identical with the original. For example, a dollar and its copy may both be folded into a paper airplane but only the dollar can be exchanged for a Snickers bar.

Success through ADP (Acronym Development Practice)

Identifying and executing an appropriate Acronym Development Practice strategy will allow the VM-Manager to demonstrate the perceptual skills necessary to name a winning program or product. This often-overlooked ability has yet to be addressed as a "needs development assessment", or NDA, in other management training programs (MTPs). Having a concept with the appropriate optimal idea density (OID) factor is an important step on the road to producing a successful program – but not necessarily the first one. The forward thinking VM-Manager will have a catalogue of acronyms at the ready should a worthy program or product present itself.

It is not sufficient to create a name as an anagram of the first letter of a series of words describing the nature of the program. The word selected has connotations both in and of itself and perhaps historically for your business. The failed Public Object Oriented Program (POOP) is a notable example. Your business may have a tradition of naming projects and products after astrological signs or planets within the solar system (being certain to avoid both Pluto and Uranus). There may be a predetermined naming convention that suggests a kinship between products that exists only on the balance sheet. There may even be a set of proscribed names that are only whispered, never written down and when spoken aloud are usually accompanied by furtive head movements and a grim and sorrowful expression. A quick look into the history of previous projects, particularly those that have failed, will assist the VM-Manager in making an informed choice.

One format presently dominates the conceptual naming space for programs and products. This convention has amended the use of one-word acronyms by prefixing them with a single letter, generally a vowel and varying its case from upper to lower as desired. Sometimes this prefix is separated from the acronym by a dash – it becomes an artistic choice at that point. It is clear to the observer that there is a relationship between like named programs and products as well as a distinction between the "i" world and the "e" world.

Forward thinking pundits in this field have readily expanded the format by employing two letters as well as introducing consonants, thus doubling the information content and further separating themselves from the pre-existing information sets. The temptation to include numeric values in this double-digit format is a trap to avoid. Adding a number will spur any perceived obsolescence by saddling the program or product with what is obviously a version number. As we all know, no one wants the first version of anything. You might start out with a value other than "1" but the immediate question is raised of what happened to the previous versions and how many attempts were there that failed.

Truly innovative VM-Managers will find a way to include an "X" in some manner as it is well know that such programs are "eXciting", "eXtreme" and "eXtrordinary" while conveying a titillating sense of danger. This consonant has the virtue of being highly distinguishable in any location – capitalized as in the preceding examples, as in a prefix "X" or even "x" and as in a suffix "-X" which would certainly find favor with Generation-X'rs.

Summary

The VM-Manager has the power to influence his own success by occupying a central position in the information flow. Careful modulation of that flow up and down the organizational hierarchy can both enhance and obscure the importance of the role she plays.

Project status materials and the accompanying review sessions provide opportunity for advancement by heralding one's own successes. Using a minimum amount of real data, these reports and sessions can demonstrate a VM-Managers' ability to handle complex projects without knowing any details in depth. A VM-Manager's business acumen is demonstrated by pouncing on flaws in other projects during these reviews. Mastery of the short-form proposal known as the "elevator speech" is another indicator of that ability.

The shift in focus from functional responsibilities to human resources responsibilities has pushed the trend toward a greater application of VM-Principles. Including non-project related tasks extends the project timeline and allows technical responsibilities for success or failure to be shifted to the team members.

The manipulation and even invention of terminology strengthens the impression of a VM-Manager's value. The use of obscure yet vaguely familiar terms gives an instant aura of intelligence to the VM-Manager using them.

The artful use of email maintains the VM-Manager's electronic presence. The contribution of these missives does nothing more than keep the VM-Manager's name appearing in the upper management's inbox. By imbuing all communications with self-assurance and self-confidence while maintaining a terse manner, the importance of the author and of the message is made apparent.

Information degrades naturally when transmitted electronically unless boosted in some manner. Processes and procedures within an organization can cause dilution without knowing it, particularly when independent groups perform tasks by rote, to separate priorities and on independent timelines. The VM-Manager can employ this knowledge to avoid unplanned failures.

Selecting the proper project name elevates the importance of both the individual and the project. Flashy names draw attention and success by association. After all, people preferred the Thunderbird to the Edsel.

MANAGING TEAMS

Launching the Lifeboat

Dear Mr. Frank and Mr. Willard —

I am a manager for a software development firm in the Southwest. We build software that provides business management solutions for a wide range of applications used in many industries. I am responsible for a team of about twenty that consists of very technical people who design and develop this software.

Over the past year, my managers have instructed me to do two things that have given me incredible grief. First, I have been required to select which team members to put on a list for reductions in staffing. This is particularly difficult given the high skill and experience level of my staff. They are all high performers so there is no good measure to apply to this task.

I am now also required to monitor project work on a first-in-first-out basis and assign it to whomever is available. This seems to satisfy management by immediately associating a name with a project, but does little to address the need to assign specific skills to specific issues. I have tried to explain to my managers how we need to consider the specialization these people have and make changes to accommodate the highest and best use of each team member. I am continually pushed back with "follow the orders given".

Having seen already what happens to those who question this policy in our company, and not wishing to jeopardize my own career, I am fearful of what will happen to me if I continue to question this policy. Is there anything I do?

Terrified in Tucson
==========
Dear Terrified —

You are the victim of a common Veneer Management practice related to viewing people as "resources" rather than as uniquely skilled individuals. This fits nicely into the VM view of the world of attaching immediate action to every problem regardless of the relevance of that action.

No VM-Manager worth their salt will ever allow a line item on their project plan to have no resource assigned. This risk occurs if the manager waits for a specific skill set to be available. In the same way, this impersonal approach allows for the creation of the termination list.

Study the concepts in our book related to Managing VM Teams for suggestions that might offer longer life for both you and your staff through the addition of titles and certifications. Read our work and learn how to identify the danger zones. And then, for both you and your team members, fasten your seat belts. It is likely going to be a rough ride.

Frank and Willard

Experience and Knowledge - What Is It Really Worth?

VM-Resource Practices have accepted the premise that experience and knowledge are no longer key factors in making assignments. Making a virtue out of a lack of resources, whether human, budget or time, the VM-Manager suspects that the moment she relies on an "expert" is when the project begins to slip from her control. In this environment the question becomes whether the Google-Web provides a viable substitute for experience. Is experience important or just an anachronistic relic?

In the VM-World, it is important that the manager not place too much emphasis on experience. Rather, adopting the attitude that a resource is a resource is a resource, the ability to assign any warm body to a task keeps the project plans and status reports in the green zone. Never forget, at the heart of any VM-Organization is found the compulsion to deliver apparent good news. This is distinguished from actual good news in that the latter implies something of substance while the "good sounding" news is motivational boosterism that is spread like fertilizer on the VM-Garden.

Geezers, Gurus and Geeks - Retiring the Old Guard

The VM-Manager uses the Google-Web to bring in possible knowledge sources beyond the Evident Information Horizon. Having information available instantaneously, on demand and in abundance has replaced the previous dependence upon Geezers and Gurus. Reliance on the relevancy and confidence algorithms of modern search engines to distill millions of references to the top 20 or 30 references supersedes the need for those who previously provided input based on experience and knowledge. Today, having a few Geezers and Gurus around will tempt the manager to wander into that dangerous terrain of having more useful information than can or should be included in a project. The requirement for actually having available the necessary skilled people to provide reality-based information, implies that the manager is actually seeking knowledge. If a VM-Manager is faced with having to deal with the G and G groups, he is also faced with the real possibility of being unable able to cover his own incompetence.

Rather than risk exposure, an agile VM-Manager will staff his team with a collection of interchangeable parts. The reason Southwest Airlines only flies Boeing 737s is due in part to the fact that every spare in the system will fit on any airplane. The same principal can be applied here by assuming that, as we just said, a resource is a resource.

Of additional note is the cost of maintaining the G and G groups. The longer you have an employee on staff, the greater his or her cost, not only in direct salary dollars to cover pay increases year after year, but also in greater benefit costs due to longer vacations and rising healthcare expense as the workers age. To truly succeed in the VM model, all the parts are expected to be interchangeable. G and G groups, with their specialized skill sets, run counter to such an approach.

Pockets of resistance to this paradigm shift of replacing G and G groups with the Google-Web knowledge collection persist within VM-Organizations. The fading levels of experience and knowledge is made apparent by the oft repeated statement "Oh, we laid off the guy that knows about that". Thus, the "search engine" is a primary enabling tool of the VM-Manager and the embodiment of the VM-Philosophy. By cleverly instructing your "resources" to use the boundless ocean of information available on the Google-Web you can successfully remove the costly and time consuming overhead of the Geezer and Guru groups.

Make a virtue out of knowing as little as possible. It becomes liberating in terms of both time and effort while eliminating those annoying know-it-alls.

Good, Better, Best - The Whirlpool of Excellence (WOE)

There are times when the shortage of staff cannot be rectified by using the Google-Web on a voyage of discovery to the Evident Information Horizon. The VM-Manager cannot predict when a project will require an additional source of high quality information and assistance. Companies operating under the Green Water Strategy address this need by creating Whirlpool of Excellence resources. These groups are designed to concentrate selected skills and rapidly review potential solutions, tools and techniques. The successful outcomes and best practices can then be spun back into any project soliciting such help.

The charter of WOE teams limits their scope to supplying a proof of concept or the occasional prototype. As they are not bound by schedule considerations outside their own environments, tying a project timeline to a product of WOE will create churn rather than forward motion. Referencing the WOE team in the project review demonstrates the VM-Manager is aware of the resource and is willing to investigate any utility the corporate body might supply. To avoid any impact to the project timeline, no dependency on this resource will be indicated nor any guarantee implied that a solution will be obtained or necessarily employed. WOE is a repository of valuable information but retrieving it in a useful manner will require the VM-Manager to have the patience of Job.

Shirts and Skins: Picking the Players

The VM-Manager must take pains to avoid being misled by a mirage of qualification. Resumes, transcripts and interviews provide a smoke screen hiding the real nature of a candidate. In today's business environment it is the ability to manipulate the artifacts rather than to demonstrate expertise in a particular field that finds the path to success. As it becomes more and more difficult to manage the excessive information of modern corporate life as well as simply land a job, displaying a colorful and confident plumage has become a desirable option.

The most successful VM-Managers build teams with similar values, personalities and life styles. While there is room for individuality, no team can survive with an excess of "characters". One way to ensure compatibility is to monitor and moderate the competency level of the team. To do so the VM-Manager must have just enough understanding of the competency categories detailed in an earlier section. You can review this information in "The Illusion of Competency".

The Science of Certification

Despite the low value VM holds for experts, there is a requirement in many professions to exhibit superior knowledge and skill through the possession of certificates. These are issued by institutions of higher learning, training academies and internet businesses to name a few. Unquestionably, there are many professions where a depth of training, stringently verified, is an absolute necessity. Doctors, nurses, pharmacists and other patient caregivers need to know what they are doing. Having assurance that the pilots of the jet airliner we are riding in are competent and have the required licenses to prove it, is a basic assumption underlying air travel. In many other industries, however, we wonder if it measures mental capacity or is just a merit badge.

The idea of "certification" has undergone a subtle shift in its appreciation. In professions as noted, holding such a document identifies the person as particularly skillful. In lesser occupations, holding a certificate may convey an idea of mystical abilities or a simple differentiator in a pile of resumes. As the Green Water Strategy takes hold, we have entered a realm where the pursuit and acquisition of credentials is spiraling out of control.

In the world of Veneer Management this situation provides a fertile field for exploitation. Certifications exist and are avidly pursued in every discipline and every conceivable sub-division of those disciplines, in every software program and even sub-functions of those programs. Niche businesses have sprung up with the sole purpose of providing the means to obtain these certificates. Instead of having a mug on your desk saying "World's Best Mom!" or "World's Greatest Grandpa!" you can have a framed certificate proclaiming you as the "Master of Pivot Tables" or "Chief Data Base Plumber" as awarded by the Data Rooter Foundation.

When considering certification one needs to view it from both the perspective of the certificate holder and from the hiring manager's view. A certification or license means something different based on which role in which you find yourself.

Team Members and Certification

The large number of people holding university degrees today has had the effect of diluting the value of these degrees. When we started our business careers, the requirement was generally a Bachelor's degree. Today, with nearly everyone in possession of this credential, it holds much less power and stands almost as a minimal qualification for many job applications. Following our entry to the workforce, the MBA became the searched for minimum qualifications of job applicants. Until very recently there remained a certain mystique attached to this degree but due to both the sheer number of MBAs roaming the planet now and the number and variety of institutions granting the degree, this too is becoming less impressive. It is not unusual to see applicants with multiple Master's degrees. It continues to grow more difficult to set oneself apart simply through the acquisition of either a Bachelors or an MBA – there are just too many of them.

The same can be said of another popular certification that has taken the world by storm over the past few years – the Project Management Professional or PMP. Like the MBA, this acronym is attached to resumes in hopes of making the candidate more attractive as a potential job seeker. Both the suppliers of the MBA and the PMP advertise how much more one will be paid with theses credentials and both frequently fail to deliver, at least in the current market.

To add to the problems with gaining these degrees and certifications, we must also include the costs associated with obtaining them. Both are pricey and in the current job market, getting a return on salary that is adequate to repay those costs is becoming more and more of a problem.

This puts the educational institutions in rather the same boat as the Wall Street purveyors of stock – the real money seems to be not in the acquisition of either stock or certifications, but rather in the sale of them. In a poor economy, learning institutions generally benefit as people search for ways to distinguish themselves from the competition.

If you are not working you may as well be in school, particularly if you accept the sales pitch that says, "you will make money from getting this". Therefore, many of us are buying these certifications, but like the stockbroker, the money goes to the salesperson not to the buyer.

Getting Past the Hiring Filter

The human resources department forwards stacks of resumes to the team leader for selection. The team leader, having one job to fill and unnumbered resumes to consider, skims each one looking for a quick way to reject them. Seeing either of these sets of three letters fosters an immediate impression of qualification and the resume is placed in the "keep" pile. Those lacking either set may or may not be rejected in this initial pass.

The VM Manager makes the assumption that the candidate possessing the MBA or the PMP designators is better suited for the position. Other less certificated resumes are destined for the shredder. The question is if this measure of competence used by the hiring manager is valid and should it also be used a basis for pay? The answer is a resounding "YES" - if the hiring party is a true VM-Manager. On the other hand, a more insightful view might be, "It depends".

Pay Me More – I'm Certified!

There are those who have the necessary evidence that they have gone through some form of training and have successfully passed the required tests. As a reward, they are granted the authority to add those magic letters. But does that actually make them the best candidate?

A VM-Manager looking to insert the most agreeable job seeker onto her team will be looking for a number of things, notably the assurance that the job seeker will not be better than the manager. That might result in the VM-Manager later being exposed as incompetent. Aside from that however, she will be looking for some measure of ability. If she also holds those certifications, she will have a very good idea of what to expect from the candidate. She will know what was required to pass the tests prior to being granted the titles and thus can more accurately predict how the candidate will react in a variety of circumstances.

151

As for the belief that a candidate is more qualified based solely on those credentials, the VM-Manager also believes in his own credentials and will, by association, believe in others with the same certifications. The result, in a predictable VM way, is a self-serving reinforcement of the myth. And thus, the "science" of certification is perpetuated.

Universal Disassociation - Cut Loose from Someone Else's Reality

The ability to separate ones' self from their surroundings is a common defense mechanism. It is employed by individuals to protect themselves against the effects of physical or mental harm and thus escape an uncomfortable reality. Standing apart from the situation allows a person to be detached from events. They assume no responsibility for those events or for their participation in them. Essentially, they become automatons that appear to participate willingly while declaring they have no control over their actions.

VM encourages this condition with its fundamental assertion of assumed equivalencies. That is, any individual within a functional discipline is identical to any other. Each one has the same utility and is interchangeable. Having developed the universal playbook for all processes and procedures and trained the staff in the techniques these documents contain, this must be so! The skill set required by the discipline is not an essential factor in assigning work. Tasks can be directed to the first person available creating an impression of responsiveness on the part of the VM-Manager and of a project that is moving forward.

However, by disparaging the usefulness of expertise, the true value of that resource has been blunted. Individuals quickly recognize when they are held in little regard and react accordingly, usually withdrawing from the project by limiting their active involvement to tasks as they are assigned.

Another factor is the ability of VM to rapidly redefine its own environment by dividing the tasks at hand into smaller and smaller pieces, then repackaging them at will. VM extends that idea to work assignments defining little or no apparent relationship between them. One task is the equal of another. Everything, eventually, has to be done so the sequence of tasks is not recognized as significant. By defining and measuring labor strictly as piecework, continuity has been removed from the equation. The introduction of a "pull" process where individuals select their own assignments re-enforces the trend. Adverse selection occurs where the harder tasks are left untouched. When what it takes to do a job is not held in high regard, why work harder than necessary?

By cutting the resource base free from a shared sense of accountability, no one is responsible for anything beyond the task at hand. The result is a universal disassociation top to bottom where leaders choose actions unrelated to the product and the workers do just what they are told, and no more - less if they can. This can have a beneficial effect on productivity by reducing the Caring Capacity Index (see *"Managing Your Career"*). Through this disassociation, the individual personally cares less about the how and why of a project and focuses on the what. The less energy you expend caring about the job, the more productive you become. We will discuss this in more detail later.

Management is not immune to this behavior but manifests it differently. Most commonly, this appears as selecting certain facts or re-interpreting those facts in a manner to support their conception of reality. The VM-Manager furthers this exercise of imagination through the selective reporting of information for review.

This works out well for the VM-Manager as force reductions become necessary to recover from this economic fiasco. Having become disassociated and disaffected, the chosen staff members are almost ready to move on saying, "I was looking for a job when I found this one." Though perhaps not willing, they will depart without remorse.

Performance Matters

A common problem for managers in business and government is what to do with a troubled employee. By that we mean, how do you ever fire someone for being incompetent in the modern world of personnel law? We understand with and agree that these laws were created to protect against any abuse of power, which results in the unlawful termination of an employee.

VM-Managers do need to remove certain employees and retain others based on their relationship to the VM-Manager's goals. One of the tools used by the VM-Manager to determine this is to put the burden on the individual in the form of the employee self-evaluation. We mentioned earlier how the successful VM-Manager will create a team of like-minded souls in order to ease the day-to-day burden of people management. The classic rules in building a team are set aside: technical skill sets, experience and ability matter far less than style, delivery and malleability. Thus, an entirely different set of values dominate the VM-World. Employee self-evaluations, aside from their obvious fictional attributes, provide a rich source of material for the VM-Manager as it requires the employee to keep track of what they have done all year and how well they did it. This avoids the unpleasant tasks of having to justify either promotions or firings, which are especially time consuming for a manager.

It is clear that the longer a manager waits before taking action, the more it costs him in time spent coaching the employee on how to improve. The rest of the team is negatively affected by the extended presence of a peer that would be better off working elsewhere. Apart from the effort needed to document a proper case for dismissal, managers simply have a hard time telling people bad news. Outside observers have commented that much of Corporate America suffers from "institutional niceness" or a failure to criticize poor performance. Early in our careers, we learned that a frank evaluation of a colleague's competency was poorly received and actively discouraged. This inability to criticize constructively results in managers and team members having to express negative feelings in less appropriate ways. Those who have lived and worked in the Pacific Northwest recognize this as Seattle is the unofficial capital of passive-aggressive behavior.

Motivate to Retain - De-motivate to Terminate

Maintaining a surface level appreciation for the work the staff performs, the VM-Manager is limited in how to motivate some and set others on the road to dismissal. It is difficult for the manager to determine whether the staff is doing a good job or a bad one except in relation to her own goals. Seeking ways to encourage the pliable and terminate the unruly - those who thwart the VM-Manager's aims - is challenging.

154

Frequent and vocal public praise is one of the best tools available to the VM-Manager to motivate those she wants to keep. It is well established that employees regard recognition, regardless of any monetary attachment, as a significant reward. It has been shown in study after study that public acknowledgement exceeds the motivating factor of money. While we suspect that VM-Managers are behind these studies, until we can do further research we accept the premise for now that praise alone pays big dividends. It further serves to create an atmosphere in which the chosen individual is less likely to seek a move elsewhere. It is a win-win for both employee and VM-Manager.

Motivation under difficult economic conditions becomes easier for the VM-Manager. With fewer jobs available, hints that staffing levels are being reviewed will tend to keep people in line. Reminding them that their bonus comes every two weeks when their paychecks do not bounce tends to limit the demands for salary increases. Handing out promotions and changing job titles even without salary adjustments usually produces a boost in intensity if not actual performance.

On the other hand, firing people is hard work. The VM-Manager is especially handicapped where the termination needs to be based on performance. Not having any grasp of the actual work an individual should do, other than generating flashy presentations and reporting positive statistics, the VM-Manager must rely on other means. Generally, this is through de-motivation where the employee decides to leave on their own. Using the same motivational statements described above but altering the tone and emphasis will raise concerns in the employee who, having any sense at all, will begin a job search. This is often where the passive-aggressive approach serves the VM-Manager. She utters subtle and not so subtle negative statements in the employees' presence. Couching lateral transfers as promotions without salary adjustments, mediocre performance reviews, small or no salary increases and a continual stream of boring assignments will bring a realization to the impacted employee that perhaps they just do not belong.

Stop Shuffling Your Feet and Fire Him!

This is not to say that a VM-Manager will never fire an employee. If the circumstances are advantageous then anyone is subject to removal.

Clearly bad employees take up a lot of time. It is important not to dither around. Having determined there is no value in keeping the employee, it is best for both parties to end it quickly.

Frequently, the VM-Manager will look for an opportune reorganization event during which to reposition the undesirable worker. Doing so precludes any need to document actual poor performance. There is a small advantage with Veneer Management in that by not depending on measures of experience or knowledge you can put an employee on the reduction in force list ("we don't need you anymore") at any opportunity. An alternate VM-Strategy is to move the individual to another team making it someone else's problem.

The typical VM-Manager will have already supplied just enough information in performance reviews, project related emails or notes to support adding the name to the layoff list while not raising any flags if a transfer is implemented instead. In any case, it is more expedient for the VM-Manager to utilize a reorg for removal instead of the more painful and time-consuming process of documenting negative performance.

The Corporate Escalator Accelerates

Eliminating staff positions is a classic way to impact budgets and improve the bottom line. The VM-Manager should be alert to an obvious means of moving ahead on the Corporate Escalator using a technique called The Cappelino Maneuver after its first observed practitioner.

Most organizations build budgets around projects that are planned for the future. Staffing projections are part of this budget. Money is set aside to fund these projects months or even years in advance. The popularity of these projects tends to diminish over time but for one reason or another remain in the budget. Though not yet activated or possibly never to be activated, they continue to show up in review after review.

The astute VM-Manager will spot such budgetary items containing unfilled and un-fillable vacancies. By recommending that all of these positions be eliminated, the VM-Manager gains immediate prestige as an economic wizard. Imaginary budget dollars appear to be saved and an opportunity for immediate advancement made available. The title of vice-president may soon to be offered to the perpetrator of this action.

Spam: A Means to an End AND a Food Group

The notion of "spam" is universal and understood by anyone even remotely familiar with electronic mail. Like the weekly supermarket ads that used to spill out of your physical mailbox, your electronic mailbox is also subject to an overflow from strange, mysterious as well as mundane sources. The personal nature of these items greatly exceeds anything you may have received from the local grocer, paint supply, hardware store or carpet cleaners. Offers to supply the hottest new medications, the fastest weight loss (or gain) programs, mail order brides and husbands and of course those pesky solicitations from Nigerian princes, appear day after day. Fortunately, businesses have found ways to protect their email systems and their employees from this constant barrage.

This focus on the grossly negative aspects of offers to teach belly dancing or how to get cheap car insurance has overlooked a large class of spam generated within any business. This internal email noise tends to fall into several broad categories:

- Social – messages from persons or groups on non-business related topics
- Organizational – messages of limited value broadcast as widely as possible
- Corporate – messages concerning activities having no impact on most recipients

The social category is clearly a reflection of the normal human need to communicate and associate with one another, and other than an opportunity to embarrass each other, has little impact. Likewise, corporate messages commonly have small impact on the recipients. Though they generally open a window into the complexion of a business, they more commonly reflect upper management speaking to each other or the outside world. Their most common purpose is in supporting upper management VM maneuvering of the type discussed

157

in *Managing the Dialogue*. Unfortunately, much time is spent pouring over the emails looking for hidden meanings.

It is the second category, the one that covers messages of an organizational nature that produces the most Corporate Spam (CS). Organizational messages create a natural medium in which spam will spontaneously generate. As these emails are usually announcements that milestones have been met or that projects have completed, a flurry of congratulatory messages appear like a flock of ducks rising from a pond. Progress status messages create less of a stir in the email network as the information they convey means little to anyone outside the project. Of particularly small value are burn down charts describing progress against outstanding tasks. The fact that the chart shows a line ascending to the right does not seem to faze the aficionados of the term "burn down".

This category is also one the VM-Manager may exploit for his own purposes. As noted earlier in "The Application of Grayscale in Communication", the VM-Manager can use the opportunities these messages create to achieve a measure of self-promotion. The VM-Manager will also send spam to his peers or members of other teams in the guise of asking seemingly relevant questions, either for information or assistance, trapping the unwary reader into doing useless work. While this can occur in both directions, a competent VM-Manager can turn the tables on the senders by including these emails as a measure of his industry and importance. Lastly, the VM-Manager can focus the attention of an unwanted team member on these emails while looking for a way to bounce him from the team.

Summary

In the Veneer Management world, experience and knowledge are viewed as less valuable than the ability to produce the perception of experience and knowledge. When it comes to your team, you need to keep in mind that you pay more for verifiable experience and knowledge but you may not gain the advantage you need to operate in a VM-Environment.

An alternative source of knowledge is the Google-Web. This access to data outside the Evident Information Horizon prevents the organization from being held hostage by a team of Geezers and Gurus. Still the VM-Manager needs to build a team that will not cause any problems and will always support his personal goals. Selecting the right candidate based on artifacts generated in a VM-Environment makes the choice problematic.

Going hand in hand with experience and knowledge is certification. While having your team made up of people with certifications attached does not guarantee an increase in knowledge or experience, it does guarantee the ability to hang a gauze curtain over the actual abilities of the team by focusing only on titles. Gaining a certificate may or may not actually bring skill with it. It may simply generate more income for the holder.

Following the practice of assumed equivalency, VM fosters the treatment of staff members as interchangeable robots. The employees respond by acting as if they were indeed mindless machines. As both groups become disassociated from the work, they escape not only from the reality of a situation but the responsibility as well.

Motivating an employee to stay on board or to resign, to retain one or to fire another, are two sides of the same VM coin. By learning to associate positive and negative Pavlovian inputs with the desired outcomes the astute VM-Manager can encourage the ne'er do wells on his team to vacate voluntarily thus avoiding the vexing problem of justifying a termination. In the same way, positive inputs will encourage and reward VM-Behavior in keeping with the VM-Manager's wishes.

Personnel changes can be facilitated by corporate reorganizations. The impetus to improve budgets through staff reductions can benefit a VM-Manager with a personnel problem. It can also be an opportunity for advancement when eliminating positions to be filled sometime in the future.

By inundating all parties, including your own team, with an overload of information you can display not only your own amazing technical knowledge but also leave everyone else dazed and confused as they wonder how you keep track of it all.

MANAGING YOUR CAREER

Launching the Lifeboat

Dear Mr. Frank and Mr. Willard –

Upon graduation from a prestigious Eastern university, I began my corporate career with a major multi-national. I have been at it with that same company for five years now and have managed to work my way up to a Director level position in the Research and Development area. The problem is, I have watched many others arrive after me and pass me by. I do not understand what it is I am doing wrong that has so slowed my advancement. Can you help?

Stalled in Sacramento
==========
Dear Stalled –

For starters, good grief! In only five years you've managed to get yourself to a Director position? We like to think the folks in those slots bring the necessary background and experience to enable them to support the teams under their guidance.

Please do not take offense at our comments, but it seems highly likely that you have already exhibited many of the traits of a Natural VM-Manager in order to have achieved this level of success in such a short time.

If, however, you still feel you should be moving further and faster, we advise you to refer to our section on "Managing Your Career" in our book Green Water Strategy. *Much of what you can do to advance yourself is discussed in this work.*

Meanwhile, whatever it is you have done to get this far this fast should probably be what you continue to do. Keep acting as if you know what you are doing.

Frank and Willard

Self-Promote Your Own Career

VM-Career practices highlight communication as a means to create an environment fraught with ambiguity yet ripe with possibility, a style of self-promotion, and a technique to create the appearance of an ever-expanding knowledge sphere. A VM-Manager desires the appellation of knowledge engineer but avoids being perceived as the expert in order to escape the inherent limitation of being type cast. It also helps to avoid the requirement of actually possessing that knowledge as well as avoiding work.

The Roman Circus - Pretend Like You're Interested

The Circus Maximus of ancient Rome was the biggest event of its day. Imagine the Super Bowl and the Stanley Cup and the World Series all rolled up into one huge event that includes roaring lions. Such a magnificent gathering would draw an enormous crowd today. It would definitely appeal to those wishing to be seen in the presence of the powerful. While an outrageous analogy, this is pretty much what a modern day Veneer Management organizational meeting amounts to, minus the lions. Replace chariot racing and gladiators with a competitive corporate show that includes self-promotion, glad-handing and mutual adulation and you end up with Veneer Management Circus Maximus.

The VM-Organization delights in putting on a show, which invariably portrays a fantasy cloaked in just enough shiny veneer to be believable. Include some flashing logos and marching bands to help focus the audience's attention. Moviegoers were swept away by the non-existent lands portrayed in the Lord of the Rings films, or more recently the dramatic locations in The Hunger Games. All those scenes of mythical settings were simply created by making real places look mysterious. They looked believable on the screen and we were absorbed into the fantasy.

It is only a small step between a movie portrayal of a fantasy world and the alternate reality of a well-executed Veneer Management All Hands meeting. Instead of humans sacrificed to wild beasts or epic sword battles, we are entertained with amusing video clips, glowing sales reports, and grandiose possibilities for future prospects. It may not be as entertaining as seeing a laser vaporize the Empire State Building, but it is fabricated with an equal amount of imagination.

When faced with attending one of these grand scale company meetings there is one thing to keep in mind whether you have signed up for the VM-Survival or VM-Success career path. This is the one time where everyone on the field is playing the same game for the same effect. Whether you are the company CEO just in by jet from Dubai to talk about the latest big project to be funded with Middle East petro dollars or you are the receptionist, the atmosphere of this meeting dictates only one acceptable behavior. Pretend as though you care deeply.

In the world of VM, these big shows are little more than award presentations for the corporate "American Idols" of the company. It is a time of self-promotion and self-congratulation with a veneer overlay of gratitude toward all those who made the overwhelming success of *<your project name goes here>* possible. The result of all this commotion is a lot of applause, much hand shaking and backslapping, and rewards bestowed on non-participants of the celebrated project. The end result is that a series of boxes are checked off on a number of management to-do lists around the company

To wit:
- Held celebration for project completion? Check.
- Award for most inspiring leadership? Check.
- Provided motivational speech for the "little people" to keep them aligned? Yep.
- Delivered a strong perception of both competence and completeness? That's also a check.

As a postscript to these events, be sure you pay a visit to your own manager after attending and drop a number of comments regarding the topics covered at the meeting. This serves the dual purpose of demonstrating that not only do you care deeply about the organization and its activities, but also you were actually paying attention.

For these events, which are nothing less than little trips into a modern day high-rise Colosseum, put on your best clothes, and by all means, be on your feet, smile, applaud and pretend as if you care. For those who

163

may choose this forum (pun intended) in which to do battle with VM, the outcome can only involve facing the unleashed Veneer Management Lions.

Minimize Your Maximum Effort

A construct exists within the world of Veneer Management that might be described as the "Maximization of Minimalization". While this magnificent alliteration seems a bit confusing at first, when one considers the deeper meaning it becomes clear that much of the activity taking place in a VM-Organization is targeted toward making the most out of nothing. At its core, VM is all about perception. Given that perception is easily manufactured out of thin air, it follows that little of a concrete nature is required to succeed in the world of VM beyond the ability to deliver a positive message.

From that standpoint, some of the best VM-Managers in the world are inspirational speakers. They have mastered the ability to put the right collection of words together to convey feelings of hope and possibility, even when the audience is composed of individuals who will never alter a thing about their lives in spite of their deep-seated intention to do so. They came to the speaker's presentation because they know they want something good to happen in their lives. By delivering words of encouragement, the attendees leave feeling upbeat and smile all the way to the door.

Similarly, a skilled VM-Manager will aim to deliver a buoyant message during his reports. For these events, unlike the Program Review utilizing the minimalist one page presentation, the more slides on the PowerPoint, the better. The fact that they contain nothing of substance matters less than the positive and hopeful feelings conveyed in the flashy visual presentation. This meets the goal of maximizing the delivery of minimal information. The less said the less accountability.

The bottom line is we all want to have hope. That is why we spent $50 billion on lottery ticket sales in the United States in 2011. In the same way, a skilled Veneer Manager can deliver a stunning presentation filled with facts, factoids, and factious fiction, the various state lottery commissions deliver us a message of hope in order to convince us to plunk down that dollar even though the odds are ten million to one against us.

Making the most out of what you have, and delivering it in a cheerful and colorful way, particularly if it involves the use of charts and graphs, no matter how meaningless, will always result in a departing audience full of good cheer. At its very core, VM is all about convincing those around you that indeed you do know what you are doing and that their dreams can come true.

Increase Your Productivity by Managing the CCI

Two VM-Concepts were identified previously as important indicators in evaluating an individual's level of satisfaction or frustration at work: The Caring Curve and The GAS Line. The earlier discussion focused on the emotional and behavioral aspects that become apparent through the interaction between the Curve and the Line. The following paragraphs expand on these concepts by defining the CCI measurement of an individual along the Caring Curve.

In biology, the term "Carrying Capacity" is a measure of a given biotic region's ability to support life. In the same way the capability of a geographic region to support many life forms is measured, we can measure the capability of an individual to support high levels of productivity in a Veneer Management business environment. To this measure, we attribute the term "Caring Capacity" and the measurement is the index or the CCI.

The Caring Capacity Index (CCI) is a measure of the Caring Curve in relation to the GAS Line. The measurement is taken in positive and negative integers to indicate the position of the Caring Curve above or below the GAS Line. (We refer to being "behind" or "in front of" the GAS line in conversation). Simultaneously, a Team Productivity Line (TPL) is also plotted against the GAS Line using the same scale of measure.

Don't You Care?

On any given project and on any given day, some team members are productive. Another group may as well have stayed at home. A third group is drifting somewhere in the middle, perhaps able to justify their pay, perhaps not.

The difference in these three groups may be based on several factors: specific skills applied at the moment, personal ability, interest in the current events and perhaps the individual's health and the state of affairs at home. The VM-Manager cannot affect most of these things. Similarly, you will be unable to influence these items through your strategy of VM-Survival or VM-Success. There is, however, one aspect of this that will play into a bigger picture of success or failure – The Caring Capacity Index. Managing the CCI can improve your personal job satisfaction and your productivity as well as that of your team.

Index Me
Scientific studies have shown there is a relationship between the individual's transitory interest in a project and the productivity level which that individual brings to the table. This seems like common sense. The more you care about what you are working on the more you will work on it: the more time will be spent in making it right, correcting each flaw, potential or otherwise, expending greater effort in the smallest details, collecting more information and trying out alternatives searching for the ideal solution. In the end, a greater effort is not equal to greater productivity.

For the same reason, the less it matters the less you will do: the least amount of effort will be invested to accomplish the task without regard to utility, purpose or other detail element not previously specified in any requirement. It is on those "low-care" days that you will find your staff surfing the internet. They are not using the Google-Web for research, but to find a hotel for their upcoming vacation.

The key to influencing the Caring Capacity is first to recognize that it exists and second to apply influences to alter it in the desired direction. While seemingly counter intuitive, a person or a team reaches their greatest potential as the Caring Curve approaches a minimum value where the GAS Line is fixed at a measure of zero. Experience will often show that the less one cares, the more productive they are. While this initially seems to not make any sense, one need only consider the effect of stress in a VM-Environment, particularly on those individuals not actively involved in VM. It can also be shown that both VM-

Managers and non VM-Managers benefit from manipulating the Caring Capacity Index (CCI). The following diagram shows how this works:

Release the Caring to Improve Your Productivity

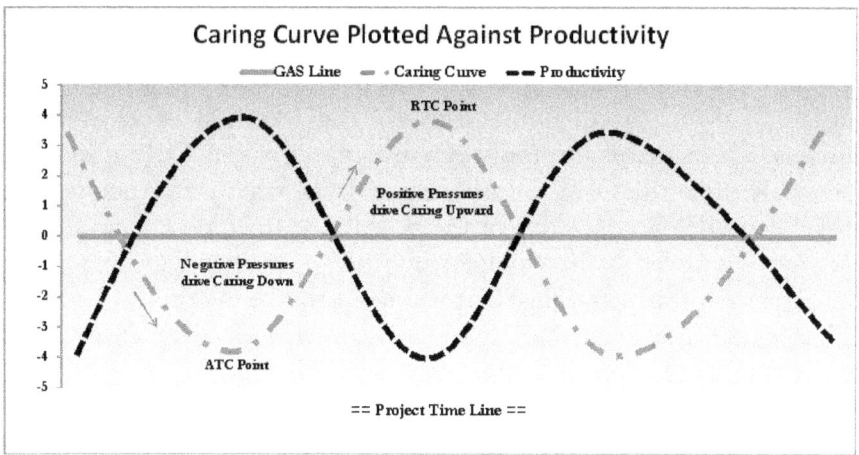

In this diagram, you will see the relationship between the Caring Curve (CC) – which is the measure of the workers current attitude toward the work they are doing - and the Team Productivity Line (TPL). The unexpected result is that when the CC is at its highest point, productivity is at its lowest. This is due to the various negative and positive pressures applied to the CC.

Positive Pressure – CC Moves Up
When the team member perceives that rational thought is being applied to their work and things generally make sense to them, their Caring Capacity goes up. Thus, the insertion of quality and performance goals, increased product values, advanced training, or technical challenges will make the individual feel good about what they are doing, but it has the unforeseen effect of making them less capable. This is no doubt due to the added energy spent in doing things that do not appreciably affect the bottom line – things like learning to use new tools and technology, digging deeper into understanding both the tools and the broader aspects of the work. There is an increased involvement, an increased expenditure of effort but movement toward the productivity goals is retarded. As the Caring Curve moves up the individual spends ever-increasing amounts of time producing nothing other than personal

growth and satisfaction. So, while the Caring Curve goes up and there are smiles on the faces of your team, they are not getting anything done as evidenced by the sinking Team Productivity Line.

Negative Pressure – CC Moves Down

On the other hand, turn loose the Department of Intentional Failure on a project, making progress seem impossible and failure inevitable, and the team stops pursuing their "feel-good" fantasy and gets down to business. As displayed in the diagram, the insertion of changes to process or standards or tools or any of the usual DIF traps will inevitably drive the team toward a more "well what difference does it make" attitude. You see this in the downward trending Caring Curve. Of note, however is the resultant increase in productivity. No more time spent on learning things that will not advance the project but only enhance the individual. Not more wasted time in "deep dives", but rather a return to Green Water where only the surface layer is being dealt with. Consequently, there is a positive move toward higher productivity.

Escalator Etiquette - When to Stand Aside on the Ride

While the world of Veneer Management is fraught with hazards, it also holds almost limitless possibilities. When considering your career, you must, as we have pointed out before, define your overall strategic objective – is it VM-Survival or VM-Success? At all times you will want to keep this strategy in mind as you navigate the shoals of the Shallow Thought World. Many reefs lie just under the surface and a seemingly innocuous route through the shallows has sunk more than one sailor in this uncertain sea.

A topic to consider in this VM-Navigation Strategy is your choice of VM-Survival or VM-Success based on your manager's objective. You may be anxious to press your successes to ensure promotion and increase your prestige, power and pocketbook, or you may enjoy living the life of the recluse, staying just out of sight and letting your contributions ensure a successfully symbiotic relationship with your nearest VM-Manager. Either way, you must consider your manager's position as you gain understanding of when to press ahead and when to slip behind the cover of a convenient wall.

Your VM-Manager Seeks Survival

If you work for a VM-Manager on the Survival path and wish to avoid finding yourself in the unemployment line, your choice is straightforward. You should support that manager in whatever quest they undertake by providing the necessary artifacts and displays needed to carry them in their chosen direction. That means reports, Power Points, status updates and even verbal praise will be required of you in this position.

If your VM-Manager has chosen VM-Survival for himself, you have the option to pursue your own objectives largely unhindered by your manager. If you are also seeking VM-Survival, you may have the best of both worlds. Since all either of you wants is to cruise below the radar, you need only operate in the "less is more" airspace and play the game alongside your boss. On the other hand, if you wish to pursue VM-Success, your manager will most gladly accept your additional input of reports and graphs and charts, as they will then be able to pass them up the command line along with effusive praise for your exceptional abilities. These actions make them look good to their manager without presenting a threat.

The only real danger in this combination is the possibility of your VM-Manager tossing you under the bus should there be a need for a convenient sacrifice. It can be difficult to predict this activity so most VM-Success tacticians in this position will pursue a rapid promotion and subsequent departure to another position in order to minimize exposure to this possibility.

Your VM-Manager Seeks Success

If you discern your VM-Manager is attempting to ride up the escalator to a higher position, your safest posture is to offer nothing that could be perceived as threatening. No questioning of priorities, no disagreement over timelines and certainly no balking at producing whatever information is requested of you. In the interaction between you and this manager, it is critical to appear as non-threatening as possible by being as agreeable and cooperative as you can. Since VM is all about perception, deliver the perception of the happy corporate vassal at every opportunity. Step aside and allow them to appear to succeed. In this scenario, you must assume the role of VM-Survival to avoid conflict. If you hold aspirations to ascend, you should put those on hold until you are able to transfer or the VM-Manager moves along.

Your VM-Manager is Not a VM-Manager

On the other hand, if you have the good fortune of working for a non-VM-Manager you have the option of exercising VM-Thinking on behalf of your own career. To complicate this, however, you will need to determine your own VM course of survival or success and adjust your actions accordingly. Without having to consider how a VM-Manager affects your actions, you will be able to proceed according to the appropriate plan for your own career objectives.

In this regard, we are particularly amused by the possibility of working for a non VM-Manager who provides you with an environment of actual, measureable success and the ability to produce genuine products. While we realize this is a bit of a pipe dream, we do believe that these opportunities, while rare, still exist. Should you be fortunate enough to find yourself in this situation consider yourself lucky and enjoy life in a world that is rapidly disappearing.

Do not be lulled into complacency in this event however, as the rise of VM-Managers is so widespread it is likely your experience will be a short one. As a precaution, we advise anyone in this situation to continue a routine study of VM and make observations in other groups and teams around you keep your VM spotting skills sharp.

Be Near for Success - On Vacation for Failure

We pointed out in our discourse on Divergent Convergence the need to understand proximity as it relates to VM-Survival or VM-Success. This is a cornerstone of the practices you will use to position yourself correctly in many VM scenarios. Much the same as being caught standing at the checkout counter of the 7-Eleven with a gun in your hand leads to the assumption you are the one who just robbed the place, geographical location plays a very large part in defining who gets credit or blame for a project at work.

A distinctive feature of VM-Managers, and something you will readily associate with Natural VM-Managers, is their uncanny ability to be seen in the company of winners. You can observe this during staff and all hands meetings when leadership is recognizing performance and the VM-Manager is singled out for his heroic contribution to a successful project. Keep in mind that the project may or may not actually be successful. It is also possible and even likely that the congratulated VM-Manager had little or nothing to do with the project. Regardless, victory is declared and other managers and company executives believe it to be true. Irrespective of the less apparent realities of the situation, the VM-Manager is all smiles as they stand and receive the accolades of their peers and the rest of the company.

No doubt you will experience something akin to frustration and even mild disgust as you say to yourself, or maybe to your co-worker sitting next to you, "That guy had nothing to do with this project". Perhaps your comment will be more along the lines of quietly pointing out to your neighbor that the advertised project is actually in a tangle on the floor and your team was called out by the client who is livid over the lack of quality with what they actually received. No matter, the project is victorious, the VM-Manager is festooned with garlands, and no doubt money, and their reputation amongst those who have the power to affect their life has never been better. You have just witnessed a demonstration of the maxim "Be Near for Success".

We also understand that the nature of VM-Business will often produce failure, either by design or through natural events. Veneer Management project plans will include numerous options for redirecting the responsibility for adverse events, be they temporary setbacks or outright failure modes. Sudden reversals of fortune may crop up in unexpected ways and at times which the VM-Manager has not anticipated. In those cases, the well-bred VM-Manager subscribes to the adage "Be on Vacation for Failure". While this does not necessarily imply the need to actually be on vacation, that is an outstanding choice to make. Whether one is disassociated from the failure through careful arrangement of assignments or by ensuring survival via the shelter of a tropical beachfront condominium, the ability to not be seen or physically associated with the failure achieves the desired result. This is known as plausible deniability in the conspiracy theory movies we love to watch, in which the high-ranking official is shielded from blame when a shady deal goes bad. It works the same way in VM-Business.

This started for us as a theory to explain how certain people seemed to always manage to collect credit for good news. After years of research and observation, it has become more of a law in the world of VM. Allow this law to positively affect your career by ensuring you are in view for success and in the shadows for failure.

The Myth of Multitasking

I recall being on a job interview many years ago the first time I was asked if I was skilled at multitasking. I answered "of course" since we all know the rule about answering questions on a job interview: unless the question ends with "and did you spend time in prison?" you always say yes. The plan is to get the job and later worry about how to support the outlandish claims you made during the interview.

Certain things you should not pretend to have experience with, but claiming to be skilled at multitasking carries only a slight risk of causing you a problem. It is commonly assumed that we all know how to do this. Living in our complex world, it has grown into an expectation and has become a typical question asked by hiring managers. We have all been trained to act as if we not only understand multitasking but that we excel at it.

The truth is, with only a few notable exceptions, none of us can actually do more than one thing at a time. There seems to be some societal dogma that makes us all believe this is one thing that is required for success. Unless you are a circus performer, you are not likely to be able to ride a unicycle and juggle at the same time. Or, as we sometimes see, drive and read the paper or drive and text. Lately, the government has figured out what a poor job we do of multitasking and has outlawed texting while driving and to some degree cell phone usage behind the wheel. This acknowledgement of our inability to multitask is at least a step in the right direction.

Multitasking Produces Multi-bad Results

Friends and co-workers sometimes challenge us when we find ourselves grumbling about the worship of multitasking being a false religion foisted on us. Their usual argument is to provide us with an example of how they needed to support two or more projects at the same time. They can always provide what appear to be sound business reasons for this, usually based on schedules, client commitments, and unexpected events that seem to leave no choice but to multitask. We challenge them to explain to us how they can be effective in that situation. The truth is they cannot. They can neither explain it to us nor provide any sort of solid evidence that such an approach is effective. In truth, multitasking has only two results – both bad.

Dilution of focus is the most notable effect of multitasking. When you are unable to put your sole focus on one item, there is no other possible outcome except "less". Less focus means less progress. It also means less quality in the result.

The other consequence of multitasking is that things take more time. Split your focus and it will take you longer to complete anything. There is no other possible result – you will require more time and you will see a poorer outcome. Always. Period.

Consider an athlete. They invest an incredible amount of time honing their skills no matter what sport. Skiing, baseball, golf, tennis – all require intense and repetitive focus. Make a note here – *focus* - single-minded, uninterrupted, repetitive and relentless focus. That is how you become an elite level athlete. Not by spending part of your time working on your golf swing then shifting to practice your butterfly stroke in the pool followed by an evening of tennis. It is by focusing – laser-like – on a single objective.

The Mask of Multitasking

There are circumstances that seemingly justify the adoption of multitasking as a means to improve productivity. This occurs when the lack of available work results in downtime. Usually this happens when waiting for an external event or for someone else to act. Earlier we discussed a VM-Precept involving complex approval processes. The existence of such a process can result in having a task parked while waiting for approval. If your task is queued up for that approval, how do you spend the time while waiting? Surfing the Google-Web? Shopping for new shoes? Or by having a second item ready to start while waiting for the first? This last solution is the common practice that opens the door to the subtle introduction of multitasking. While waiting for task one to gain approval you begin task two. However, as certainly as the sunrise, you will soon be waiting for both items one and two. Then what do you do? You add item three.

At some point, the number of concurrent and partially completed projects in your queue will exceed your ability to manage them. Clearly, this is outside the control of the individual doing the work since all activities are in a hold state while awaiting someone else's input. Regardless of how this develops, time will be lost as the worker struggles to recall what it was that was being done as each items returns to the active queue. Time passes, memory fades, and notes are incomplete: different decisions and choices are made changing what happened before items were set aside

Meetings and Multitasking

Another way we end up with multiple tasks lies in the promises made by the VM-Manager while attending meeting after meeting. In each meeting, a list of work items is discussed and the VM-Manager, struggling to maintain their competent appearance, makes promises that end up being assigned as multiple items for each of their team members. In this scenario, one day of meetings can easily result in every team member being overloaded with tasks that can only be managed by multitasking. Another feature of this unregulated task spawning method is the false expectation generated around task completion, as the promises made in these meetings will include delivery commitments.

Multitasking as a Perception of Good

So why are we even bringing up multitasking in this book? It is because we have identified multitasking as a key component of Veneer Management. It accomplishes the one thing most important to the VM-Manager – it generates the *appearance* of progress. Because you are working on six things at the same time, your manager can report up their chain of command that each of those tasks is in process and moving ahead. While you may understand that all six tasks are suffering because of this dilution of your effort, you have to admit it does provide for a nice progress report up the escalator. Remember, it is never about what actually comes out the end of the pipe, only that we can see something moving within the pipe. Multitasking supports this madness.

One final aspect of multitasking in the VM-world needs to be pointed out. There exists a subset of individuals who are not only ineffective at multitasking; they take the mismanagement of multitasking to a new level. These people exhibit a form of BSOS – the Bright Shiny Object Syndrome we discussed earlier. You will recall the original treatise on BSOS examines it from a VM-Manager perspective and identifies it as the constant distraction new and interesting concepts bring to that VM-Manager. In a slightly different way, some individual workers are subject to a multitasking induced BSOS wherein they are continually distracted by the variety of tasks in their queue to the extent that they can never finish any of them. Repeatedly drawn to the most interesting aspects of any single item assigned to them, these people will shift from one task to another based entirely on the momentary attraction of a work item.

From a VM-Survival or VM-Success perspective, it is critical for you to remember that a positive attitude about multitasking be presented publicly in all cases. Unless a revolution takes place in the business world and this myth of multitasking is challenged and eventually eliminated, you must learn to operate in such an environment. To succeed you need to be a proponent of this approach, offering it as a solution brought to the table when projects are stalled and in trouble. To survive you need only chant the phrase "of course I can multitask" whenever you are asked. Under no circumstances should you ever allow yourself to challenge the approach.

I Have a Pivot Table Fetish

Pivot tables are a fact of life in the world of Veneer Management. Any competent project manager will find multiple useful ways to total and sort and redisplay any set of data imaginable. Remember that a base concept of Veneer Management is to say the same thing as many times as possible in as many ways as possible to maximize the sense of value that accompanies receipt of a very complex looking report. To the recipient, even unintelligible data has immense value, particularly if it can be displayed in multiple nifty ways.

Utilizing the pivot table function of Excel allows the crafty VM-Manager to provide multiple views of the same data. Often, with a well-constructed pivot table, the redisplay of the data through an alternative view actually has the ability to redefine the content of the data. This fits perfectly into the concept of VM-Data-Display and redefinition.

Interestingly, our investigation into the use of Excel pivot tables as a redefinition and display tool led us to a completely unexpected yet related topic. Based solely on the word "pivot", our research uncovered a closely related concept we want to include here. For this discussion, we point to the definition of "pivot" as "rotate, revolve, or turn". This applies to our initial interpretation of the pivot table allowing the VM-Manager to "turn" a perception of displayed data into the desired comprehension, but it further allows us to consider pivot as a completely new VM-Concept.

Doing the VM-Pivot

In basketball, pivoting is important as it defines the planted foot around which the player is able to redirect his energies away from the defensive opponent. The same applies to hockey when you see a defender skating at full speed in reverse as he faces down the onrushing puck carrier, only to somehow change direction entirely and in an instant, transfer all his speed and energy in the opposite direction as he pivots on his skates. This is akin to the pivot we see in Veneer Management. A sudden and complete redirection while losing no speed and draining no energy. The VM-Pivot.

Be on guard for the VM-Pivot as it can put you in much the same position as that hockey player we just described. You may be skating along on that thin skin of ice, feeling like you are in complete control and seeing your career moving along nicely, or you may feel you are in safe zone and are very comfortable with your job when – BAM. The VM-Pivot knocks you on your back.

There is no known way to predict this event. While we have studied it at length, we have only succeeded in identifying it as an unpredictable phenomenon, much like an earthquake. While you are much more likely to be the victim of a VM-Pivot, it is also possible for you to be the initiator of this action. Be aware that the outcome is not yet fully understood so taking action to initiate a complete change of direction in your career can have unpredictable consequences.

We have identified the VM-Pivot as being associated primarily with shifts between VM-Success and VM-Survival tactics although we have not yet ruled out the possibility that there are other causes.

Identification of the VM-Pivot as an operational phenomenon has given rise to the newest concept in Veneer Management.

The VM Subduction Zone

Wikipedia says this about subduction zones –

> *In geology* **subduction** *is the process that takes place at convergent boundaries by which one tectonic plate moves under another tectonic plate, sinking into the Earth's mantle, as the plates converge. These regions are known as "Subduction Zones".*

The theories related to the discovery of the VM-Subduction Zone represent the very latest in VM-Research and VM-Thinking.

We have said much in this book about VM-Success and VM-Survival and the need for every student of VM to select one path or the other as a strategic objective. We also mention the need to be able to shift selectively between these two choices in a tactical fashion in order to support your overall strategic goal. Keep in mind that your strategy – the big picture – may require shifting tactics to reach your ultimate goal.

VM-Subduction-Zone Theory states that at any given time, a tactical shift may be required between VM-Survival and VM-Success in reaction to events. The stress caused by this shift has the potential of causing unanticipated effects. These effects seem to generate from the natural physical stress exhibited between the two realms – VM-Survival and VM-Success – and may result in temporary movement away from the desired strategic direction.

Modeled after the understanding of plate tectonics, VM-Subduction-Zone Theory interprets and explains stresses induced by rapid and dramatic shifts between the two VM-Strategies in terms of the resultant effects generated by such an action.

VM-Subduction-Zone Shift from VM-Survival to VM-Success

For an individual who must react to an unexpected event causing the need to assume VM-Success tactic as a temporary Protective Measure, the introduction of stresses can be great. To understand this scenario, imagine an individual who has assumed VM-Survival tactic and has been following that course for some time. Unexpectedly, this individual recognizes behavior from his VM-Manager that indicates an upcoming sacrifice may be in the works and indications are that our VM-Survivalist is to be the victim. In this case, it is entirely appropriate for this individual to take action to ensure long-term survival by temporarily adopting a VM-Success tactic.

In this case, the threatened employee may suddenly take on a very active role in promoting himself, attending many meetings, participating vocally, making recommendations and generating copious information to promote his cause. This will have the desired effect of creating a perception of competence and thus offer a measure of protection that is intended to derail the VM-Manager's plans for a human sacrifice.

While the desired short-term outcome of this tactical adoption of the VM-Success Tactic may be met, the sudden shift from the prior non-involvement of the actually intended VM-Survival mode will leave many feeling shaken. Co-workers in particular will find themselves asking, "What the heck is this guy up to?" This is the beginning of the seismic shift induced by the unexpected redirection of the endangered employee's VM-Strategy. This has the potential effect of registering as a major quake, noticed by nearly everyone.

Upon successfully avoiding the intended beheading, the prior assumption of VM-Survival Tactic can be resumed and the employee will return to a quieter and less active lifestyle. The impact to co-workers at this point is minimal as they see the intended victim resuming his expected behaviors.

VM-Subduction-Zone Shift from VM-Success to VM-Survival

Likewise, events may occur that cause a person previously on a VM-Success course to shift tactics to "stay out of the line of fire". Typically this shift causes much less anxiety among others and can often pass entirely unnoticed as the move to slip behind the curtain and avoid any expected bad outcome produces fewer noticeable waves. In this case, it is rather like a micro-quake that passes largely unnoticed. From this perspective, the VM-Success to Survival shift operates in much the same way as "being on vacation for failure". Out of sight, the potential negative effect is less likely to be felt.

So new is VM-Subduction-Zone Theory that we have yet to develop fully tested responses which we can recommend. Having seen the negative outcomes to individuals trying to shift from VM-Survival camouflage to a temporary VM-Success Tactic, we can only caution you to be on guard during this period. We look forward to your sharing of results in this area in order for us to increase the knowledge base of VM in future publications and trainings.

Summary

Veneer Management organizations know how to put on a good show. Since it is all about delivering an image that we interpret in a positive way, creating a well-received performance is one of the hallmarks of the mature VM-Company. Just be certain you do not rain on the parade and dissolve the thin film of perception. And wear your best clothes.

You can only care so much, and there are times when you frankly do not. That is the time you become aware of the GAS Line and all it can do for you. Get on the wrong side of it and your world can go up in flames. Knowing when not to "give a shit" is a critical component of your VM-Career.

Managing the Caring Capacity Index goes hand in hand with positioning yourself safely in relation to the GAS Line. Productivity, paradoxically, is inversely related to the CCI. Learning how to influence and interpret the CCI will ensure your continued survival and offer you the opportunity to succeed beyond your dreams.

While success and the ride up the Corporate Escalator may not be on everyone's agenda, understanding when to hop on for a trip and when to take the stairs is a critical piece of information for anyone operating in a Veneer Management universe.

Standing next to a winner can only be good for your reputation. But then there is the old saw about "guilt by association". At times it is best to be out of the office when the ice melts and your skates grind on the concrete floor. Learning how to time your exposure and disappearance is a valuable VM-Skill.

Do not be misled by those who seem to think you can do two things at once. Multi-tasking turns out to mean working nights and weekends because you have been co-opted by two teams or assigned to two simultaneous functions. Learning to recognize the signs of this myth will help you steer the ship away from the reef.

"Pivot" has become a popular word in use for politicians. It is a euphemism for the more pedestrian phrase "flip flop". Regardless of the term you prefer, in the world of Veneer Management, a change of position equals a restatement of "fact" in order to justify a current position. Just as we watch our political candidates support and then denounce a particular policy depending on the audience they are addressing, the brilliant VM-Manager will become skilled at directional shifts.

Finally, when it comes to your career, if you don't get what you like, like what you've got.

CONCLUSIONS

Don't Hate the Player

The cast of characters in this passion play include the employees, the mid-level managers, the senior managers and upper management. In other words, everybody. The old adage was that one was either part of the solution or part of the problem. If you become a victim of Veneer Management you might simply be part of the scenery, or in this case a cog in the machine, doomed to rotate on the work-a-day shaft with no relief in sight. Embrace VM and you can ride the tsunami of failure right up to the beach of success.

Without an appreciation of Veneer Management, the individual courts a career of frustration in an attempt to make sense of the organization, its on-going purpose as well as its day-to-day behavior. Morale will suffer as will commitment and eventually your performance will decline with an accompanying stalling of promotions and raises. In this environment, the open door policy very well may be the exit that leads to the street.

For all of their monolithic properties, corporations inevitably promote an image of being open to change. By not understanding the utility of variability in priorities, in processes, and in scope, management appears indecisive when it is merely exercising its flexible, nimble, agile nature. The individual will embark on a quest for a reason behind the change but that quest will not be satisfied or will end in disillusionment. The sense of "change is good" and "change is a part of life" is less important than impressing on a superior that you are ready and willing to respond to any change that strikes their fancy.

Whether Veneer Management is in play or not, it is a well-known fact that the mid-level manager enjoys the worst of both worlds. They are the conduit for corporate messages to their staff and must often pass on the most unpleasant messages with no indication of dissent. Conversely, the staff will try to send similar messages up the line which the mid-level manager must mediate as the senior managers have no desire to hear about problems the mid-level manager has not already solved. These individuals quickly seek out VM-Principles without even being aware of the term simply as a protective mechanism.

The mid-level managers will also seek out the path of least resistance when faced with process and procedure changes. Experienced managers realize that all such elements are malleable given the limited time the senior managers responsible for such changes will be in their positions. They become adept at manipulating information so that only positive impressions can be formed. They will also appropriate credit for any success within their reach in hopes of moving from one position to another.

Senior managers must demonstrate some level of understanding of the projects which they sponsor. By applying common methods of status reporting, they can be assured of grasping the salient elements by keying on the predominant color on the chart. They also standardize the terminology so that communications between themselves and their peers and with upper management share the same terms. In America, green is the color of a good status report as well as that of money.

On The Outside Looking In

Our purpose in this book is to help those of you who, like us, were mystified by the behavior we witnessed in our organizations as we struggled to understand the thinking behind choices from the decision makers.

Veneer Management, like it or not, is here. It has already penetrated the boardrooms and executive suites of countless corporations and it has overwhelmed the agencies of government from local to national and international levels. We have, for the first time, attempted to examine and explain the broad range of symptoms exhibited by the agencies expounding The Green Water Strategy. We have provided theories to explain the sometimes unexplainable, developed tactics for dealing with the fallout created by these organizations and offered you direction in how you react and respond to scenarios in which VM is affecting your life.

The names we have assigned to these theories and concepts are our own. No company is going to name their Department of Intentional Failure the Department of Intentional Failure. It will be something like Product Development or Consumer Affairs or some other innocuous title that reveals nothing of the real purpose. But you get that – you have been shown how to identify the activities of VM by our examples. You now know that when a project seems to have been torpedoed and sunk in spite of every evidence of potential success, you have seen a DIF-like organism at work. And while they will not call it a Pure Failure, the result will be the same.

As you paddle quietly through the shallow Green Water world, looking for a secure direction to steer, make note of the actions of others – both your peers and your superiors. As you observe their behaviors, you will learn to recognize the effects of a Shallow Thought Mindset, be able to identify a set of proposed actions that outline a Green Water Strategy and see evidence of the Cosmic Stupidity Cloud. Travel slowly through these waters, looking in all directions and drifting carefully.

Throughout this work, we have reminded you that your choice is generally one of two options – either survival or success. Either choice requires stealth. By applying what you now know, you will be much better equipped for moving quietly toward or away from every VM encounter.

Survival or success. The selection of one of these paths will be your primary goal, but you will find that both will be appropriate for you on a case-by-case basis. For example, suppose you are a software engineer, keenly enjoying the challenge of taking a complex customer requirement and turning it into a coded solution. You harbor no interest in riding the up escalator to a team lead position. You want nothing to do with all those personnel and management reporting headaches. You want to remain exactly where you are. The reasonable conclusion in this case is to pursue a VM-Survival course.

On the other hand, if you are anxious to move up the Corporate Escalator and assume a more prestigious title, you will assume the veneer of VM-Success. This approach will require you to measure your day-to-day activities in light of how they will appear to those with the power to direct your future. Steps to improve your appearance of competence need to be taken. Following the directions provided in this book, you will be able to provide the appearance expected and know how to generate the requisite views of your projects and your progress.

As you increase your understanding and awareness of Veneer Management, you will likely detect its presence through the behaviors we have discussed in this book. However as you begin to note the presence of VM, do not assume you will be able to communicate your knowledge and perceptions to everyone in your company. Many of them will remain unaware of the existence of this new business paradigm. By bringing it up you may appear to others as if you have taken leave of your senses. You must be cautious in your conversations, ensuring that those you wish to include in your discovery are carefully tutored to reach the same conclusions as you. A good solution is to provide them with a copy of this book.

Consider the information presented here as a framework. We do not have all the details since there are so many possible permutations of VM induced activity. The topics we have covered are intended to provide the broadest and most general coverage for the greatest number of readers.

The discovery and description of Green Water Strategy and Veneer Management is recent and, as a result, we are still very early in the process of studying and understanding it. As the first to undertake an up-close review of the practices of Green Water and VM, the authors are working to refine information into more specific knowledge. As part of this work, the authors have founded the Veneer Management Institute. This group is dedicated to the study of Green Water Strategies and the activities associated with VM. See the Appendix for more information on this organization.

EXCERPTS: GREEN WATER STRATEGY MANUAL

The following are items extracted from the Green Water Strategy Manual. This manual provides more detailed information about the topics covered in this introductory book and offers further discussion of the underlying theories and principles of Veneer Management. This manual is still in the production phase but availability is planned for 2013.

The topics selected for presentation here have been previously mentioned and are included for quick reference.

Micro-Segmented Marketing

Market-share is the Golden Fleece, the Holy Grail of every modern business venture. According to VM, this slavish adherence to the macro-economic approach overlooks opportunities that do not require the resources of a mega-corporation. In fact, in the environment of the mega-corporation, these opportunities are often overlooked for that very reason – to the VM-Manager, they simply do not appear complicated enough. The combination of modern technologies and social fads can be a productive source of new and exciting, if somewhat mercurial ideas. The forward thinking Veneer-Manager will mine his or her staff for these nuggets, polish them with imagination and mount them in attractive settings on the fast track to success. Having an insight into the growing a-communal nature of the twenty-first century labor force, which is paradoxically joined with a constant need for connection and by rampant consumerism, the VM-Manager can possess the formula for certain success.

For example, the establishment of desktop computing has fostered the idea of a "programming" cottage industry. This is secondary to the notion of working "at home" and in opposition to the corporate approach of offshore computing. It ties into the human psyche at an egocentric level where everyone believes they can produce the great American novel or the next killer app or the next viral video.

Indeed, the present generation of computing and network access via handheld devices has created a global market for applications of an extraordinarily personal nature. Thousands of apps are available to the consumer, many of which have a life span not much longer than a fruit fly, and are often just as useful. Personal customization of these apps stresses direct human involvement as their key feature while suggesting that each individual can and should contribute to the global cache of worldwide information.

The personalization of these devices and the applications running on them creates a demand keyed at an individual level identified through micro-segmented demographics. This is similar to the way political parties tailor their messages to special interest groups and Political Action Committees. It is now an everyday occurrence to be inundated by targeted advertisements while surfing the web or to be handed a sheaf of coupons by the clerk at the checkout counter when leaving the grocery based on your purchasing patterns. There are a myriad of apps available to battle those annoying pop-ups and a host of eager app developers and their managers dedicated to producing a product you must have for any hope of evading them.

 Further, through the application of the Law of Large Numbers, even tepid interest in these products can produce monetary gains. For example, there are over 5.6 billion cell phones in the world of which the US has nearly 327 million. That is more than one per person. (Other nations also have more phones than their population – Hong Kong has nearly twice as many cell phones as citizens; China and India are closing in on a billion phones.) Sales of .01% would be 32,700 in the US and 560,000 worldwide. Even a rate of .001% would be 56,000 worldwide and at $5 a pop would be $280,000.

Surely, given an interesting name, sexy packaging with an inviting price, someone somewhere will purchase anything once. Besides, the author can always say they are diligently working on a super new product rather than whiling away the hours playing video poker in their mother's basement.

Patent Trolls -Why Bother to Create?

SAN FRANCISCO -- Google lashed out at Microsoft and Nokia in a regulatory complaint, accusing them of illegally feeding mobile patents to a technology troll scavenging for billions of dollars in licensing fees that threaten to drive up the prices of cellphones and other wireless devices. -- Michael Liedtke, Associated Press, June 2, 2012

A manifestation of the Green Water Strategy can be found in its approach to product development. Maintaining a robust R&D organization requires a large budget, significant staffing and up-to-date, high-tech facilities. As one finance executive put it, "We don't make money writing software." Indeed, the money is clearly in sales and lots of them. Such costs become a target for reduction through the Green Water Strategy.

In the modern business world, ideas come very fast - it seems like a thousand a minute. You see evidence of this by turning on your television and flipping through the channels, especially late at night. It seems that every gadget, device, product, service and concept is being hawked on channel after channel. You might assume that a large organization stood behind each of these products dedicated to nursing ideas from conception through development and maturation into a product destined for the consumer. The truth might be quite different.

As you think about your business, whether you are writing software, manufacturing airplanes, installing car stereos or practicing the janitorial arts, there are many opportunities in each field for new inventions. These can take the form of actual physical products, of product designs, or new or improved processes and techniques. When one considers the proliferation of cell phones and their sophisticated operating systems, it is clear just how many ideas can be turned into "product" just by browsing the market place listings on your Android or iPhone. The majority of the ideas behind these gadgets, devices, products, and services are protected, to a degree, by patents.

Under the influence of the Green Water Strategy, a different approach to R&D is taken. A GWS business is motivated by a desire to benefit from the discoveries of others with a minimum amount of effort and thus expense. Creating a Patent Troll is an ideal way to achieve this goal. The approach is to search the list of new patents in the related field and look for gaps. By filling in the missing pieces with enough arcane language and a drawing or two and you are on your way to muddying the waters and gaining credit for an idea you probably dreamt up during half-time at last week-end's football or basketball game. It all adds up to a minor effort with little or no resource cost.

Here is a perfect example of an opportunity missed. I invented the inflatable basketball shoe. To be clear, I came up with the idea some time before Reebok released the revolutionary Pump Shoe in 1989. Following that, inflatable sport shoes became all the rage. This idea came to me while I was hiking with my twelve-year-old son. We were lugging full backpacks up the southeast shoulder of Glacier Peak in the Washington Cascades, climbing out of a deep valley to intersect with the Pacific Crest Trail and were tired, hungry and our feet hurt. I began describing to my son how nice it would be if I could just inflate my boots. That would ease the pressure my feet while painfully working to gain the elevation we needed. What I did *not* do was apply for a patent on the idea. If I had, no doubt I would be a wealthy man today instead of a corporate runaway.

A GWS business will craft a Patent Troll program tailored to its particular field of interest. There are several basic elements to be included and these apply equally to a sole proprietorship or a mega-corporation:

- Apply for patents on literally everything you can possibly imagine. It matters less what the specific idea or product is than it does to cover as broad a spectrum as possible.
- For every idea, develop multiple "Near-Alternatives". The patent office will accept an idea if it is notably different. If you file a patent for a red-colored automatic wine bottle opener, you will not be able to obtain a different patent for a blue-colored automatic opener.
- As a general rule, consider using the Splatter Approach. In hockey, the more pucks you throw at the net the more goals you are likely to score. The same applies with being a Patent

Troll. The more ideas you register the more likely you are to succeed.

- Develop a strategy for monitoring markets that might develop your idea. Nothing is worse than coming up with a good idea that gets developed and you miss finding out about it. Those people in the office surfing the internet – maybe they are not just looking at porn.

The final point, the finding out about it, is the key concept of the Patent Troll activity. Remember – and this is very important – being a Patent-Troll has nothing to do with (a) being an ugly beast that lives under a bridge (or in the corner office) or (b) being an inflammatory internet lurker that annoys the rest of the universe by inserting unpleasant comments. A Patent Troll is patterned after the method used by anglers who fling a lure out and drag it through the shallows of a stream to see if a rainbow trout can be coaxed to the surface. If I had only taken the time to develop an actual concept for the pump shoe and bothered to file it with the patent office, I would have possibly been eligible for some portion of the very generous pie created by the introduction of pump-to-fit shoes. The fact that I did not bother to try and actually produce the product would not lessen my legal rights since I claimed the idea first and registered it through official government channels.

After you have expended just enough energy to establish a title to a good idea that seems likely to pique the interest of someone else or by another company, you simply wait for them to do the work – to do the designs and prototypes and plumb the markets for possibilities. Once you see the end product headed for the consumer shelves, contact your attorneys. Then you wait for the money to start rolling in. By doing so, you will avoid the missed opportunity of inventing the pump shoe and then watching someone else cash in. Stake a claim then reap the rewards.

CCI – The Double Helix of Productivity

Job performance and thus productivity are affected by the level of personal involvement an individual invests in their job. A balance is necessary to maintain an enjoyable life-style while expending just enough effort to reap the benefits of employment. Computer models can predict the point at which productivity of the VM-Manager's team can diminish or increase with accuracy.

In this model, two lines are plotted which weave around each other and against a central axis: one is the measure of productivity against plan; the other a measure of team member commitment and morale identified as the Caring Capacity Index or CCI. The central axis is the GAS Line with the direction of left to right nominal calendar time. Multiple factors contribute to this index including project time lines; number of hours worked; weekday versus week-end assignments; overtime; training requirements; organizational stability; vacation scheduling; promotions; and actions of the DIF, to list the most common elements.

As a project begins, the CCI is high, starting well above the horizontal axis, while productivity is low, beginning below that axis. Over time the CCI and the level of productivity begin to approach each other. The apex of the Caring Curve, the highest value attained by the CCI, represents the time during with the team members care the most about what they are doing. It may persist for a period of time but is commonly transitory. The instant the Caring Curve begins its downward slope is called the RTCP or the Release The Caring Point. There is a complementary position on the graph below the GAS Line at which time the team members begin to feel more positive about their work. This is called the ATCP or Assume The Caring Point and signals an upward trend of the Caring Curve.

We have implemented a rating system similar to that used in rock climbing. For example, Class 1 is walking on a sidewalk. Class 1.1 is climbing a stair. Class 5 is vertical that requires a rope to ensure safety (if you fall bad things happen). Class 5.5 requires something stuffed into a crack to hold you up.

So, applying this model:

- CCI Pos = 2.0   2 measures away from the GAS Line. Have just arrived at this point
- CCI Pos = 2.1   2 measures away from the GAS Line and have been at this point for 1 time measurement
- CCI Neutral = 0.0   Have just arrived at the GAS Line; there is no associated time measure
- CCI Neg = 2.1   2 measures below the GAS Line and have been at this point for 1 measure. Can also be stated as GAS = -2.1 (note CCI measures are both positive and negative integers and indicate the relative position to the GAS Line not to time)

We can further refine this by assigning a relative measure for the first integer – i.e. 2.0 the 2 represents a relative distance from the GAS Line like a minimum of 1 a maximum of 10. So a 2.0 is much closer to crossing the GAS Line than a 9.0 but does not consider time. For 2.0 the zero measures time of just arrived. A 2.1 would mean you are 1 time unit from the GAS Line.

When using V-Model analysis in a retrospective, projects which fail to raise productivity to match expectations consistently exhibit high CCI values. Where productivity has risen dramatically, it is accompanied by a precipitous drop in the CCI. The point at which productivity begins to accelerate explosively is where the arc of the CCI and that of the measure of productivity intersect. Mathematically and psychologically, as the level of personal attachment and commitment to a project decreases beyond the strict specification of any and all tasks, the more productive the team will become. By stripping away any extraneous elements not directly called out in the plan, the team is not distracted by such things as system performance, usability, consistency of design or any other factor not explicitly called out in the project plan.

The VM-Manager need only be familiar with this model and recognize the role to be played in minimizing the CCI values for the team. Often the DIF can be of assistance in this effort by introducing random elements such as mock audits, safe driver training and mandatory off-site meetings with executives.

In the final analysis, it is astounding to realize that the less you care the more productive you can be.

PERSONAL BACKGROUND

You may be wondering, "Who are these guys and what makes *them* think they know anything?" After reading this book, you now know one of the central tenets of VM is presenting a competent appearance in the face of a lack of actual knowledge or experience. Is there anything to prevent us from simply "acting" knowledgeable? Absolutely not! The truth is that sadly, we actually do understand these concepts from years of personal experience – and years of frustration.

The Authors

D. Wayne Willard was born a hillbilly in a small southern Missouri town before the invention of the cell phone. He brought this non-technical background to the business world after a stint in the Blue Water Navy, a failed career as a rock star, and an attempt at being a forest ranger before he finally found work as a software engineer and project manager. With degrees in Wildlife Biology and Computer Science, he brings twenty-six years of corporate exposure and ten years of government experience along with his formal education to bear on the topics in this book.

T. Barrington Frank arrived in the world as an Ohio Buckeye but was dragged by his parents to Southern California where he dreamed of becoming a professional baseball player. Suffering from the sting of rejection by the major leagues, he instead unleashed his creative energies working for several companies as an insurance underwriter, and as a software developer and manager. With a BA in History and years of painful corporate experience, he provides a unique view of the appearance and growth of Green Water Strategy as observed over four decades of change.

Having worked so many years in Corporate America, both authors have both extensive experience and formal training in various aspects of both technical and personnel management.

A Word on Writing Styles

If you were to ask Tom, he will tell you that I write like a hillbilly. To which I respond, he tends to write like a college professor. When we first started talking about the possibility of collecting this information into a book, one of the topics of concern to us was this diverse approach to words. We decided to try a few different things, writing alternate sections, each of taking a section, selecting areas by specialty or experience, but in the end we simply started writing based on the next topic in the list and which one of us was available. This was a true VM-Approach.

As the ones who reveal the existence of Green Water Strategy and Veneer Management to the world, I suppose it is fitting that some of these principles on which we report were determined by our own experiences. The end result is that you will still find certain parts of this book that clearly belong to one or the other and the style of the writing is difficult to not notice. But surprisingly, a large portion of the work, having been reviewed and rewritten by us both, has assumed a thin veneer of blended style that makes it difficult for even us to remember who originally crafted it.

For the distinctive pieces that retain our unique voice, we beg your indulgence. This is a complex subject, much of which is still in the early stages of investigation and much of the explanation we offer is still highly subjective. Over time, as the study of Green Water and Veneer Management matures to whatever thin understanding it ultimately achieves, much of this subjectivity will disappear. Or perhaps not. I suppose it depends on just how deeply anyone chooses to explore the topic.

GLOSSARY

Acronym Development Practice (ADP) - The process of creating a referential term using the initial letters of a phrase, product name or project.   Examples are NATO, Scuba, and Radar. In the business world, it is typical for a company to develop a lengthy list of acronyms (LLA) that a new employee is required to learn (RTL) in order to understand both the conversations taking place at meetings (CTPM) and the overall business strategy (OBS).

Actualization Value Optimal Idea Density (AVOID) – A measure of the practicality of any concept where a high actualization score is desirable; items with a high OID and a low actualization value have high AVOID values

Amalgamated Action Retirement Policy (AARP) – An approach used to avoid project delays due to the presence of unacceptable risks. This is accomplished through assignment of unmitigated risk to the next project. See also RCMP.

Antithetical Singularity (AS) - The appearance of less-than-human intelligence. Will occur when VM-Managers are fully in control

Assume the Caring Point (ATCP) – Nadir of the caring curve when the caring capacity index reaches its minimum. When an individual or team cares the least.

Bright Shiny Object Syndrome (BSOS) – (1) That condition which seems to afflict most upper level managers. It relates to the inability to focus on any task to completion so long as something else is available to think about. (2) An inordinate reliance on information presentation tools such as graphs and charts condensed to a single sheet or screen of data, preferably using the RGY color scheme; where data is plotted on X and Y axes, the desired direction of success is clearly labeled.

Caring Capacity Index (CCI) - A measure of the RTC curve in relation to the GAS Line.

Cheshire Cat Effect (CCE) – Condition identified with those persons who generate concepts more quickly and more often than can be captured and realized

CHIMERA – A mnemonic device which describes a testing methodology available to VM-Managers; it supports the minimalistic approach to verification while offering assurance that some amount of effective testing has occurred.

Cosmic Stupidity Cloud (CSC) – Variously, an interstellar or on occasion, a local atmospheric phenomenon, which tends to adversely affect the intelligence levels of persons en masse. The effect can be periodic as well as long-term and is not altrered by the intrinsic intelligence of the individuals affected.

CSC Threat Level – An indicator of the risk potential to effective decision-making when considering the measurement of the Cosmic Stupidity Cloud as Optimal, Low and High in combination with the Optimal Idea Density (OID) of the topic in hand.

Deep Dive – A business philosophy supporting the collection of large amounts of data to be used in decision-making processes.

Degrees of Stupidity – A VM definition of native intelligence and the ability to apply it to practical activities.

Department of Intentional Failure (DIF) - That corporate or government department specifically responsible for ensuring the successful prevention of either (a) an actual undertaking or start of a project (b) the successful completion of a project or (c) the perception of an actual failure of a project to either start or complete.

Department of Intentional Failure Teams (DIF Teams) – The group of individuals assigned responsibility for managing and administering the activities of the Department of Intentional Failure. This group is of variable size and composition, entirely dependent upon (a) business area (b) company size (c) project number and size and (d) organization structure. For companies operating with a formal Project Management Office, or PMO, DIF teams may be incorporated into that structure or operate as a separate entity. For most government organizations, the DIF Teams are modeled on NSA (National Security Agency) structures.

Divergent Convergence – The Principle of Divergent Convergence defines the ability of an individual to maintain conceptual agreement with two distinctly dissimilar and logically antagonistic views

Escalator Etiquette – In VM, the activity analogous to "climbing the corporate ladder". The distinction lies in the lowered effort necessary to use an escalator instead of a ladder.

Event Horizon Effect (EHE) – Condition identified with those persons who produce concepts that collapse under their own weight. Can also be applied to those times when an individual enters a protected zone beyond which there can be no effect on that individual from any negative outcome; related to implementation of Failure Failures through the DIF.

Evident Information Horizon – The boundary surrounding the collection of all that is known relative to a particular topic; information beyond this limit is unknown but potentially accessible via the Google-Web interface.

Failure Failure (F_F) – The technique used within the DIF of applying a specific Prevention Tactic to a project in danger of not completing by engineering the required set of events and/or reporting processes to mask the actual and factual state of affairs at the moment of consideration.

Give A Shit Line (GAS) – A theoretical line around which one's relative attachment or detachment to a project, process or other item can be measured in terms of engagement. Generally, being behind the GAS line implies a detachment from the current work or activity to such a degree as to remove any negative emotion.

Google-Web – VM reference to the use of the internet as an information source to replace skill and experience lost to terminated workers.

Grayscale – As applied to communications in Veneer Management, the intentional obfuscation of information to simultaneously create ambiguity and enhance the reputation of the VM-Manager.

Inertial Determinate Point (IDP) – During early project activity, when the team is attempting to overcome stasis and begin moving the project ahead, the VM-Manager must decide if they are taking the Survival or Success route. That point at which enough momentum has been achieved to see project planning and scheduling taking place is the IDP, at which time a course selection must be made as it determines future behavior of the VM-Manager.

Law of Decelerating Returns – The more layers of management inserted into an organizational structure the less return for effort is observable, eventually resulting in not just a decrease over time of any measureable factor (i.e. productivity, profit, customer satisfaction) but an actual downward passage of the "Zero Line".

Law of Retrograde Productivity - The state attained when one has achieved such a high degree of success that they have increased the expectations of others regarding their capabilities. This produces the unexpected result of the assignment of ever increasing amounts of work until the point is reached that the worker is unable to perform to expectations. This state continues until failure is unavoidable.

Less Information Faster Technology (LIFT) – Any set of electronic tools which enable the distillation and summarization of data and displays the results in a manner that can be interpreted at a glance; the objects generated through LIFT are commonly referred to as "dashboards".

Management Bling – See BSOS; also information presentation tools, new devices, new methodologies, new languages and new data base technologies.

Maximization of Minimalization – Less is more. Do more with less. Knowledge is overrated.

Management Training Program (MTP) - Any institutionalized process whereby existing management staff manufactures new managers in their own image. Variously known as VM-Cloning, VM-Clone, Mini-VM.

Natural VM-Manager – Persons instinctively drawn to the practice of Veneer Management principles as a means of self-preservation in a struggle to maintain a perception of competence; these individuals are responsible for the introduction of VM in an uncontrolled manner.

Needs Development Assessment (NDA) – The assumption of the need of additional information as part of some activity.

NERD Effect - Not Even Remotely Doable ideas having extremely high AVOID values.

Not Quite There Factor (NQTF) – A measure of completion of any project calculated from a comparison of the completed tasks or function points to the sum of tasks or function points defined by requirements and user expectations; used in the calculation of project drift.

Optimal Idea Density (OID) - The Optimal Idea Density or OID is a measure of complexity of any idea taking into account written and verbal communications, the nature of the concepts surrounding it and the people both presenting and receiving the idea.

Particle Duality – As applied to the interpretation of the state or status of any project in Veneer Management, the careful manipulation of messages, documents and reports to encourage the comprehension of that project that coincides with the observers' preconceptions.

Point of Incompetence Trigger – (PIT) That event which leads the VM-Manager to conclude that the project has reached that stage wherein the manager lacks sufficient capacity to continue to provide a perception of progress or success. This is the point at which DIF activities will be commenced.

Postulate of Harmonious Recombination – An axiom applied with VM that allows opposing views to coexist as a single solution. See Divergent Convergence.

Prevention Tactics – Those activities necessary to redirect an effort from its perceived natural course in order to generate a perception that matches either initial or prior expectations; widely misunderstood as associated with Risk Management which it is not: a component of DIF F_F Implementation.

Project Drift – A measure of scope creep introduced by lengthening time lines and the associated increase in user expectations.

Pure Failure (P_F) – Initiated by the Department of Intentional Failure with the intention of causing a project to fail on command. This will take place in spite of any actions on the part of the project team to the contrary.

Quick and Dirty Methodology (QaDM) – An impediment to artifact production often encountered in the quality assurance phases in which insufficient documentation is produced to support a standard VM masking model.

Release The Caring Point (RTC) - Apex of the caring curve when the caring capacity index reaches its maximum. When an individual or team cares the most.

Retroactive Validation (RV) – The rationalized testing approach that avoids potential resource drains due to excessive testing times through use of the just enough criteria that states "It worked before; we didn't change it so it must work now." Also referred to as the "grandfather clause".

Risk Condition Minimalization Program (RCMP) – A Veneer Management risk mitigation approach in which the least amount of effort can be expended in producing the most amount of supporting documentation as to why there are no risks or how any risks that exist have been dealt with in the project. See also AARP.

Shallow Solution – The VM-Approach to problem solving that stresses the application of minimalization in both design and development.

Shallow Thought – A generalized term applied to the Green Water supported application of less intensity, less activity, less expense as a part of any business process.

Shielding Actions – Those activities undertaken as part of either (a) a Pure Failure (b) True Failure or (c) Failure Failure intended to protect executive level positions from implication in any action that might be construed as having had a part in the project failure.

Unified Field Theory – As applied by Veneer Management, the reduction of any set of relationships or collection of processes to a single, uniform definition, or of any series of events with a single explanation which mandates a single, predefined solution.

Universal Disassociation – A state of mind reached by management and staff through the practice of Veneer Management; it describes the weakening and eventual severing of the personal connection to a project, team or corporate entity.

V-Model – Enabled through any combination of the principles of Veneer Management which result in a cul-de-sac contretemps known colloquially as "You can't get there from here!"

Vegas Principle of Random Success – Expresses the rationale behind employing a questionable practice, methodology or process with the expectation that an instance of prior success, regardless of how distant in time, will somehow occur again.

Veneer Management (VM) – A collection of management practices and principles based on the minimalization of knowledge and experience and applied across broad based mid and upper level management groups with the intention of enabling rapid position shifts as needed for either product development projects or damage control activities.

Veneer Management Institute (VMI) – The Veneer Management Institute. The educational organization developed for the dissemination of information around the topic of survival and success in the new world of Veneer Management. Also the issuing agency for the professional credential VMP.

Veneer Management Professional (VMP) – Certification issued by the Veneer Management Institute to those who have successfully completed a course of study and examination for the VMP credential.

Veneer Management Project Management (VM-PM) - A general term applied to those activities around project management as conducted within the VM-Environment.

VM-Charter – A project charter that modifies the generally accepted concepts for project definition in such a way as to accommodate Veneer Management.

VM-Clone – See Management Training Program.

VM-Data-Display – The process of reformatting data into multiple views that will provide differentiated interpretations depending on the presentation and the audience.

VM-Life Style – This term is applied to individuals who utilize VM-Principles in their day-to-day behavior with a particular focus on the presentation and preservation of an image of competence and success in all that they do.

VM-Linguistics – The branch of Veneer Management studies that describes the implementation of VM Information Theory with regard to communications and especially terminology; expresses through the manipulation of language the ability to define and redefine terms to suit the situation.

VM-Meeting – Conducted with the idea of provided perceptions of success rather than actual success; typically not convened for the purpose of conducting business.

VM-Philosophy – The overall concept of a thin layer of appearance in lieu of time-consuming or complex and involved processes.

VM-Pivot – A sudden and complete directional change from a VM-Success or Survival mode to the opposite, usually as a result of a shift in current conditions. (See VM-Subduction-Zone).

VM-Practices – Activities described as associated with the implementation of The Green Water Strategy in a business.

VM-Process – A repeatable set of steps intended to support any activity that is a part of the larger practice of Veneer Management.

VM-Principle – Rules governing the implementation and practice of VM as applied under the Green Water Strategy. An example is the principle – "If you don't fail you succeed." These are desired to be true, and attainable, but are faced with opposition that challenges their realization.

VM-Precept – A rule governing an activity undertaken in the pursuit of Veneer Management. It is expected to always be true.

VM-Scheduling – The process of altering schedules and completion dates as need to ensure the interpretation of a success.

VM-Subduction-Zone – Interprets and explains stresses induced by rapid and dramatic shifts between the two VM-Strategies in terms of the resultant effects generated by such an action.

VM-Success Tactic – The general application of knowledge relating to Veneer Management principles as used to further one's career, thereby enhancing both status and stature as well as providing a means to pursue an upward trajectory in one's career path.

VM-Survival Tactic - The general application of knowledge relating to Veneer Management principles as used to promote the retention of the practicing individual. This approach requires the ability to operate within a VM shroud wherein the individual protects his position by mastering the art of delivering a positive impression.

VM-Technique – A methodology by which a VM-Principle of VM-Precept is included in processes.

Zero Line - That point at which a measure of productivity is no longer increasing but remaining constant.

APPENDICES

Appendix I
Willard's Rules of Software Engineering

Willard's First Rule of Software Engineering
Adding more engineers to a late software project makes it take longer.

Willard's Second Rule of Software Engineering
Effort estimates will always match exactly the number of days management makes available to complete a project up to the point at which work begins, at which time available days are reduced by thirty percent.

Willard's Third Rule of Software Engineering – (a.k.a. Occam's Antithetical Razor)
When offered two competing programming solutions that produce the exact same results, the more complex one is the most likely to be coded.

Willard's Fourth Rule of Software Engineering
The relative skill of a coder is inversely related to the amount of time that coder expends in telling you how talented they are.

Willard's Fifth Rule of Software Engineering
Complexity and grace are not mutually exclusive.

Willard's Sixth Rule of Software Engineering
Success is in the eye of the beholder.

Willard's Seventh Rule of Software Engineering
Newer does not mean better. Better means better.

Willard's Eighth Rule of Software Engineering
Documentation is for people with weak memories.

Willard's Ninth Rule of Software Engineering
The existence of knowledge as to how to fix a problem does not authorize an environment in which we are assured of the creation of the problem.

Willard's Tenth Rule of Software Engineering
The existence of manual procedures to avoid predictable failure ensures predictable failure.

Appendix II
Willard's Corollary's, Theories and Principles

Willard's First Corollary – Facts are for people with small imaginations.

Willard's Second Corollary – Lowered expectations produce higher performance.

Willard's Third Corollary – Older may actually be wiser. Experience counts.

Willard's Fourth Corollary – Just because we can, does not mean we should.

Willard's Theory of Software Estimation - Time and engineering staff are flexible only to the extent that there is never enough of either.

Willard's Enduring Principle of Initial Development - Real Programmers do not invent, they copy.

Appendix III
The Godfather's Truisms

We are never done; we just stop working on it.

60,000 function points – they can't all work.

It does not pay to do the right thing.

No good deed goes unpunished.

Do not do me any favors.

We have not done our job if we haven't made it complicated.

Never apologize. It's a sign of weakness.

Say every other thing that comes to mind.

Making work for other people is our number 1 product.

People keep inventing bigger and better fools - Idiots are somewhat constant.

Your bonus comes every two weeks when your paycheck doesn't bounce.

Make "NO" happen – i.e., make no changes ever.

When in doubt, don't. In fact, just don't.

Appendix IV
The Voices of the Experts

90 - 90 Law
The first 90% of the software takes 90% of the time to build, and the last 10% of the software takes the other 90% of the time.

Dunn's Obscuration Theory
Visibility solves 80% of all problems.

Hofstadter's Law
A task always takes longer than you expect, even when you take into account Hofstadter's Law.

Sturgeon's Revelation
Nothing is always absolutely so
-or, put another way-
Ninety percent of everything is crap

The Law of Increasing Complexity
Simple programs never work the first time. Complex programs never work.

Wirth's Law
Software gets slower faster than hardware gets faster.

Appendix V
Veneer Manager Categories

What type of Veneer Manager are you? There are many types and gradations of manager and each merits its own classification. Each has different strengths, weaknesses, and usage in different situations. They range in value from economy to luxury, in appearance from dull to highly polished, and from rough surfaced to smooth.

Veneer Classification	Identifying Attributes	Principle Example
Balsa	VM Managers in this category are generally novices, having a soft surface knowledge of VM principles over a light-weight structure of hidden inner strengths, allowing them to bend easily but are not durable over time	M.Bachman S. Palin J.Edwards
Bamboo	The Natural VM-Managers are mostly found here. It is the fastest growing group and appears in every industry. It is popular with the environmentally minded but as they are not formally introduced to VM, tend to be rigid and though durable can be brittle if pressed against the grain.	R.M. Nixon R.Paul R.Santorum
Cottonwood	Another common category represented by a hard exterior over a soft interior. Though committed to VM, the nuances of Survival or Success have escaped them. These managers are coarse and of low value, producing little energy and though able to resist outside influences for a time, tend to crumble in the face of adversity	G.W.Bush H.Cain R.Perry
Maple	The VM-Manager in this category has internalized the VM principles and executes on them daily. He is versatile in that he can generate success in any work-a-day role and has begun the ride up the corporate escalator.	N.Gingrich J.Boehner S.Pelosi
Oak	While the previous category may be the work-horse, the Oak VM-Manager is the jockey. Not only executing on the VM-Principles, this manager is actively extending those principles exclusively in pursuit of VM-Success	J.F.K T.Roosevelt
Walnut	The first of two executive level categories, VM-Managers in this category have arrived at the top of the first corporate escalator. They feast on the efforts of the subordinate categories and mold them according to their on-going strategies.	B.Obama M.Romney
Teak	This is the top category in the classifications. These individuals have reached the pinnacle of VM and have the whole forest of VM-Categories working for them.	L.B.J D.D.Eisenhower

Appendix VI
Earn your VMP through the Veneer Management Institute

Are you tired of feeling left behind in a dead-end job with no future? Are you looking for a way to get on your corporation's corporate escalator and begin your advancement? Or are you stalled on the that escalator wondering what is going on and who hit the stop button on your career?

Would you like to take the step that jump starts your career and propels you into the future? Isn't it time to make the change that maximizes your paycheck and your opportunities? Are you tired of feeling left out – of feeling like you just don't fit?

Then it is time to check out the Veneer Management Professional Programs through the Veneer Management Institute (VMI).

Our patent-pending training in Veneer Management Science can be the answer to your dreams. For those managers floundering in an ocean of information, finding themselves totally at sea with today's technology, VMI can lead you to safety through an understanding of the Green Water Strategy. Learn to appreciate the value of the Shallow Thought mindset and how by applying the tried and true technique of maximization of minimalization you can be perceived as the success you have always wanted to be. With just enough effort on your part you can begin or resume your rise to the top.

We offer leading-edge training in beyond leading-edge management theory taught by over the edge professors. From this program you can earn the Veneer Management Professional Certification – the VMP. Our unique approach to the sciences of project management, personnel management, and process management brings together the leading experts in these fields providing decades of experience and delivering the revolutionary new concepts developed by our on-site staff. This training is not available in stores or at your local university.

Don't wait. Don't let this opportunity pass you by. Contact the Veneer Management Institute today!

Appendix VII
VM-Everything

It is unlikely, more likely impossible, that you did not notice our habit of appending nearly everything with the tag "VM". We originally intended this to provide a bit of levity in what might otherwise be a dreary topic. As it turns out it is more necessary that we imagined given the specific definitions words take on when used in this modified context.

We have included the complete list in this appendix, just in case anyone wants to review.

VM-Activity
VM-Approach
VM-Based
VM-Behavior
VM-Business
VM-Career
VM-Categories
VM-Charter
VM-Clone
VM-Cloning
VM-Company
VM-Concept
VM-Criticism-Mode
VM-Data-Display
VM-Environment
VM-Garden
VM-Information
VM-Lifestyle
VM-Linguistics
VM-Management
VM-Manager
VM-Methods
VM-Methodologies
VM-Navigation
VM-Observer
VM-Organization

VM-Objective
VM-Personality
VM-Philosophy
VM-Physics
VM-Pivot
VM-Plan
VM-PM
VM-PM-Planning
VM-PM-Planning-Activity
VM-PM-Project
VM-Practices
VM-Precept
VM-Principle
VM-Process
VM-Project
VM-Project-Management
VM-Project-Manager
VM-Program
VM-Promotional-Mode
VM-Resource
VM-Research
VM-Scheduling
VM-Skills
VM-Strategy
VM-Student
VM-Subduction-Zone
VM-Success
VM-Survival
VM-Survivalist
VM-Tactics
VM-Technique
VM-Thinking
VM-Theory
VM-Thinking
VM-World

Appendix VIII
Green Water Strategy / Veneer Management Site Map

VM Hierarchy	VM Science	VM Operations	VM Methods
VM World	VM Information Theory - Evident Information Horizon - Greyscale Communication - Greyscale Information Exchange VM Linguistics VM Mystique/Mythology VM Philosophy VM Physics VM Research - Business Model - Cosmic Stupidity Cloud - Degrees of Stupidity - Optimal Idea Density - Pivot - Project Inertia - Subduction Zone - Unified Field Theory of Management - V-Model of Failure	VM Project(s) VM Project Management - Charter - Life Cycle - Planning - Project Reviews - Quality Assurance - Risk Assessment - Scheduling - Validation - Verification VM Training - Clone - Management Training Program (MTP) VM Based Products - Increase complexity - WOE Teams - Work for other people	VM Approach - Aiming for success - Dynamically define Done - Failure Mode Management - Make Agile your friend - Schedule manipulation VM Criticism Mode VM Promotional Mode
VM Business VM Company	VM Thinking - Access to information is better than experience - All entities exhibit VM personality traits - Certification is as good as real experience - Competency is an illusion - Documentation makes anything true - Equal training means equal ability - Multitasking is necessary - Quality is the result of a Documented process - Shallow Thought Mindset	VM Categories - Balsa - Bamboo - Cottonwood - Maple - Oak - Walnut - Teak	VM Communication - Managing Up the Hierarchy - Managing Down the Hierarchy - Greyscale Messaging - Terminology VM Data Display VM Reporting

VM Hierarchy	VM Science	VM Operations	VM Methods
VM Organization	VM Principles - Any project status is subject to interpretation - Consensus (buy-in) is key - Done equals today's state - Failing faster brings success more quickly - In ambiguity lies Opportunity - Inclusion (get all opinions) - Newer Technology is always better - Perception is as good as the real thing - Random Success ensures repetition	VM Objectives - Ensure the perception of success - Expend the least amount of effort - Failure viewed as Success	VM Practices - Acronym Development - Amalgamated Action Retirement Policy (AARP) - Cappelino Maneuver - Corporate SPAM - Develop Improved Measures (DIM) - Lack of Growth (LOG) - Risk Condition Minimalization Program (RCMP)
VM Layers	VM Precepts - Complex approval steps ensures quality - Complexity increases Value - Do 'just enough' - Do less faster - Projects never end, work Is just suspended - Tools will solve every Problem	VM Strategy - Micro-segmented Marketing - Survival - Success - Tactic(s)	
VM Manager		VM Activities - Hiring - Firing - Managing e-Presence - Meetings - Patent Trolls - Prototyping	
Natural VM-Manager			
VM Teams		DIF	
VM Student			
VM Observer			

ACKNOWLEDGEMENTS

We owe acknowledgement for inspiration to a long line of managers, supervisors, co-workers, CEOs, CIOs, CFOs and other C-whatever-O's, some of whom inspired us with their skill, sensitivity and savvy. To others we owe thanks for the lessons learned of what NOT to do.

To those brave souls who allowed us to coerce them into reading early drafts of this work we owe a special thanks. You endured confusion and conflict and gained our thanks.

To Glen O'Conner who naively agreed to apply his long corporate experience to this project. Your input was beyond value but we still ignored things you said that we did not like.

To Professor Dr. Lesley Larkin for those early editorial comments, why did we ever think we could write a book and only focus on the topic? Your attack on our insensitivity regarding pronouns was only one of the many improvements you brought us.

To Dr. Colin Dean, a physicist who viewed software as a sub-atomic particle collection and built his programs accordingly. His inspiration resulted in the engineering rules found in the appendix.

Thanks to Jen M. Schell for creating the concept of BSOS and CCI and allowing us to include it in this work.

To my partner in this effort, Rev D. Wayne Willard, BS., PMP, on whom I can depend for a telling insight, a cogent theory and a pithy comment - and 1000 words on any topic. To T. Barrington Frank for sharing my distorted view of the world.

Special thanks to Suzanne for her endless support of my efforts to transfer my thoughts from brain to page. Without you I'd still be spinning in the VM-Dryer.

Cover photos by Jamie Keffer.

INDEX

Contact us at veneermanager@gmail.com

www.ingramcontent.com/pod-product-compliance
Lightning Source LLC
Chambersburg PA
CBHW051451170526
45166CB00001B/201